Colours of The Light

Stories and Lessons
for our Times

SG Williams
BSc.(Hons) RAc.

Copyright © 2023 Heart's Discovery

All rights reserved.

ISBN: 978-1-7775584-7-5

DEDICATION

I am dedicating this book to my husband Howard who likes me to read these stories aloud and wanted me to share them with others.

CONTENTS

	Acknowledgements	i
1	ANGELS' FOOTPRINTS	Pg # 9
2	THE BOYS	Pg # 19
3	ENOUGH	Pg # 27
4	INIQUITY OR INEQUITY?	Pg # 37
5	JERUSALEM HILL	Pg # 47
6	JUST SAYING	Pg # 57
7	THE LIGHT KEEPER	Pg # 69
8	OH CANADA	Pg # 81
9	HAL & OWEEN	Pg # 93
10	STARGAZER	Pg # 101
11	THE TEACHER	Pg # 111
12	WHISPERERS	Pg # 123
	About the Author	Pg # 135

ACKNOWLEDGMENTS

I thank my husband for his love, patience, support and incredible insight.

1 Angels' Footprints

Theresa was just thirteen weeks pregnant with her third child. Her other children were two and four years old. She had dropped them off at the daycare near her house, before leaving for work as a full time research associate. She was using her lunch breaks to take catechism lessons at the large cathedral nearby. She had finally decided to join the Catholic church after years of prodding by her husband. Her own family was protestant and she was not terribly religious. Her husband wanted the children to be baptized and attend Sunday school in his own faith. Theresa decided it was time and an elderly priest visiting from Scotland had offered her Catechism classes. Father McLeod had been recommended by a coworker who was a member of the Blue Army. This was a group devoted to the virgin Mary and what they believed were the authentic teachings of the Catholic church. Her colleague urged her to accept the priest's offer.

There was a lot to learn and Father McLeod had given her books to read for homework. Her husband worked shift work and most, if not all, of the child care fell on her. The bus ride home and to the daycare, provided a window of opportunity before she picked up the kids to do some studying. Today Theresa was reading about angels and demons and was having a hard time digesting the information. She was a scientist and very analytical. She did have faith in God and Christ but that was because of a strange experience she had before she met her husband. She had been travelling the United States on the back of an antique Harley Davidson with a friend, at night, when they were involved in a bad accident on the interstate. She prayed as the bike slid on its side, as if in slow motion, pleading to be spared. She was not harmed and in the events that followed she became a believer.

Now Theresa was reading about the Catholic view of other worldly spirits that only came in two types, angels or demons. Anything she did read about the Roman Catholic faith had to have the stamp of the imprimatur, according to her work colleague. The angels she read about were well documented in the Bible but did not always appear with wings as one would expect. Catholic doctrine says that they are pure spiritual beings made in God's image, created to serve God with an intellect higher than that of humans. They do not have a physical form, are neither male or female but can interact with people in human bodies as a temporary state. There are nine different choirs of angels ranging from Seraphims to Archangels that act as messengers, protectors, healers, guides and intermediaries for God. They say that each of us has a guardian angel as a protector from the time we are born.

Demons on the other hand, have the same characteristics of angels such as immortality. They are considered "fallen angels" that were once good but turned away from God and became evil by their own choices. Satan is the leader, an actual being that commands legions of fallen angels. These malevolent spirits try to separate humans from the gifts, grace and benefits of God by appealing to the weakness of our human nature. They mislead humans through the senses, the imagination and by fooling them with false miracles and by impersonating good angels. These spirits work in the shadows and don't want us to know their true nature. Their tools are accusation, confusion, trickery, lies, temptation, deceit, seduction and disguise. They try to depress, discourage and demoralize us. Then they pretend to be good and convince humans that demons and the devil do not exist.

Both angels and demons are under God's domain and are given the knowledge and scope of activities as God permits. Theresa was learning all this a number of years after she and her husband had left behind a church that turned out to be abusive. Now she had been experiencing strange paranormal attacks. A man verbally accosted her on the bus and she could see the image of a wolf overlaying his face. She found muddy footprints on her living room window and the TV kept turning on by itself. Inexplicably, a pile of boxes just flew apart and came crashing down. Then her husband and she shared the same frightening nightmare about bats. She confessed her concerns to Father McLeod. Instead of allaying her fears, he was solemn. He was not surprised and believed her wild stories. He told her that evil entities do exist and will attack. He told her she needed the protection of the church.

After Theresa's conversion to belief, she had experienced the influence and damage caused by evil entities from surprising sources. While the supernatural events were recent and new, she had felt oppression inside her previous church. She was made to feel that she was a lesser human being because she was a woman. Then when she spoke up about concerns of abuse of power, they tried to convince her she was lost to sin and an agent of Satan. They used the entire congregation to gang up on her to try and break her spirit. She left and recovered but others would appear to try and accuse her of wrongs she never committed, say things to doubt her self worth or confuse her about her faith. Whatever the source, strangers, coworkers or even family, Theresa became better at recognizing their work. Theresa believed angels helped her combat evil but could not be sure until recent years.

It was during one of her lunch breaks after her class with Father McLeod, that she met two older people while eating her paper-bag lunch, at a park bench. They noticed Theresa coming out of the basilica and assumed she was a like minded religious. The man and woman looked to be in their 60's and said they were visiting from Europe. They introduced themselves as missionaries, asked her about herself and then told her about all the places they had travelled for work. They had been in almost every part of the world. They talked about the spiritual condition of people in various countries and in particular, they were worried about the people of France. They were kind and encouraged her in her faith. They told her she was on the right path but that she had to be careful about her baby. There was a dangerous gas in her laboratory but not to worry, everything would work out for the best.

It was in the mindset of the reality of the supernatural triggered by her catechism classes, that caused her to ruminate over this discussion with the kind couple. The more she thought about it, the stranger it seemed. Their insight into the spiritual nature of so many people around the world was incredible. Then she calculated the number of of places they had been and the amount of time at each place. She estimated them to be over 600 years old. That was impossible. Then she reflected on their love of God and concern for others, their enthusiasm for the spiritual journey and the way they encouraged her in this direction. Their desire for good was infectious. Then she wondered if they were indeed angels and if so, what were they trying to warn her about in the lab? They did not make her feel worried or afraid and assured her everything would work out, but she needed to look into it.

She was not yet showing and had not told her co-workers that she was pregnant. She decided to tell a couple of women she trusted and asked them about any dangerous gases. They were somewhat alarmed and told Theresa that one of the anaesthetic gasses that she was working with was notorious for causing miscarriages, even in the wives of men who worked with this particular gas. This was not a widely shared piece of information so Theresa asked her supervisor. He said it was only a theory and that there was no proof. Theresa was upset by this news and began doing some research on the topic in the medical library. There were some papers saying that the gas in question affected cell division in the embryo. She told her employer that she would no longer work with that gas. He was understanding. They could switch to something else.

A few days later, while walking on her lunch break, she was overwhelmed by a ominous feeling about the baby. Deep in prayer, as she walked, she pleaded with God to protect the child. Then sensing that a miscarriage was imminent, she negotiated with God. In a deep sense of loss for a child that had not departed, she felt acutely sad for co-worker Claire and her husband. They had been trying for years to have children without success. The deal she offered, as she felt grief wash over her, was that she would accept the outcome if she must, but use her pain and loss as an offering, if God would give the childless couple a child of their own, in place of the one she would lose. She had already named the child and told her children about the pregnancy. Now she wished she hadn't. That evening her husband had to rush her to the hospital, where she miscarried, losing the child who was to become Kyle.

It would be years later and Theresa would always remember Kyle. He never left her psyche. It was two years since she had her classes and joined her husband's church. She still worked at the same job with Claire in research. She still wore the scapula and a blessed medal of Saint Michael given to her by the old priest to protect her from demons. When she became pregnant again, she waited at least three months before announcing it. Her boss, the principal investigator, agreed she should stay away from exposure to the damaging gas. He and another co-worker had repeatedly exposed themselves to the same gas and both their wives had multiple miscarriages over the years. Theresa could never see the good in what happened, except for the hope that now God would bless her with a gift of a healthy child this time. Everything went well.

Theresa went on a six month maternity leave, with her new baby and was able to be home with her other children over the summer. They joined the local canoe club and the four of them spent the summer at the beach. It seemed to go so quickly and by September, she was back at work in the lab. She was surprised however to learn that Claire was off work and would not be back for a few more weeks. It seems that her church had found a child for her and her husband to adopt. Claire was on maternity leave at the same time she was. Theresa was thoroughly pleased but as she learned the details she was dumbstruck. The birth mother had given up a little boy by the name of Kyle who was born in the same week as her new baby. Not only had God heard Teresa's prayers but he blessed both she and Claire. For Theresa, the name and birth date of Claire's child was an indisputable sign of a miracle.

If those two kind missionary travellers had not tipped Theresa off to a possible miscarriage, she would not have had the opportunity to petition God in the way that she did. By knowing ahead of time, she was able to prepare for the emotional loss and try to do some good with an impending tragedy. She could have been angry with the travellers and with God over the idea of such a loss. Instead she chose to accept

God's will and make peace with whatever might happen. As a result of her willingness to trust God, her prayers were answered in this dramatic and beautiful way for Claire, herself and others. Theresa researched the gas and its effects on pregnancies and then presented her findings to the other scientists in her department. Her supervisor and male co-worker were convinced, avoided the gas and both their wives were finally able to successfully bring a child to full term.

Theresa believed that the two travelling missionaries were indeed angels disguised as an elderly couple. Their encouragement persuaded her to take the high road and not to lose heart. As a result she and others were greatly blessed. The children brought great joy to all four families because of the plot instigated by a couple of angels, who delivered a message with such skill as to warn and encourage at the same time. Their depth of understanding, in her talks with them was so deep, it was almost incomprehensible. These were clearly highly intelligent and extremely loving beings. Theresa was herself smart and educated but she only managed to grasp the gist of what they explained to her. The angels did not expect her to understand, Theresa's only job was to trust God. Theresa could feel the impact of their loving presence years later.

This one encounter not only taught Theresa about the pure loving superior nature of angels but how they work behind the scenes. As humans, we cannot begin to understand what angels know. They instantly acquired their spiritual revelation, the moment they were created. Humans must acquire such insight through a lifetime on earth, processing experiences through our physical brains. The angels however can plot marvelously complex conspiracies, for our good, as we remain oblivious as to the why of life events. However if we are astute, we may see the results in the way you met the love of your life at a party, invited by a friend of a friend, for example. Or the near miss of an accident in a snowstorm. It could even be the mysterious scent of burning incense, while writing about angels. If curious, trace your life history. You may be able to detect footprints of angels in the wonderful blessings of your life.

2 THE BOYS

The new family was delighted. After three years of trying, they brought home their healthy baby boy. However they had not chosen a name yet because they dared not jinx the process. Martha had experienced two miscarriages and they had become discouraged. The grief of losing a child not yet born takes with it the hopes and dreams. They had been heartbroken before. They had not even set up a nursery. All the baby things were stored away in the generations old farmhouse. This was a special and joyful day. This baby would join the menagerie of other newborns on an acreage that had become a hospice and rescue for wild animals. In particular they had a wolf cub staying in the house. It was discovered after the mother had been hit by a car. It needed to be hand fed and had become very demanding. Now the happy parents had their hands full with the two infants.

These two little ones, Scotty and Freddy, grew up together as buddies. Before long they could run around the yard and explore the rest of the farm. They were both a bit mischievous and loved to scare the chickens. Not in an obvious way but they would lay low near the hen house and make low growling sounds. Before long the chicken were panicky, clucking and flapping their wings. The pigs were not as much fun because they would charge them and they were usually the ones to become intimidated. The pigs could be mean and bite and it was easy to get cornered in their pen. The cows did not get ruffled and pretty much just ignored them, the cats would just move to a higher perch and the old mare would just kick, sending them both scrambling for safety. The hen house was the best place to cause excitement at the least amount of risk.

They were able to go undetected until the family noticed a decline in egg production. The adults tried changing the lighting, the food. Some of the hens were culled and new ones were added to the flock. They even resorted to playing soft music. Finally the rooster, that was supposed to help the hens feel safe, was removed to the lower yard near the brook. They thought perhaps that particular male had a personality disorder and was the cause of the hen house stress. The two friends continued their antics all summer undetected until the mother forgot her basket of a couple of three eggs, all she managed to find. The boys went to the hen house when she left but did not anticipate her prompt return. Just as they growled and feathers started to fly, the mother walked in and caught them. Mother yelled at both Freddy and Scotty.

The message was clear, at least to Freddy, that they had been bad and that they were not to do that anymore. Scotty however, did not seem to get the message. Every day he tried to enter the hen house and Freddy would have to distract him by finding something else for them to play at. Scotty loved to play in the little fort that the father had built behind the garage. It was on a platform off the ground and they kept their outside toys in it. Freddy would find one of the toys and lure Scotty there where they would play games for hours and forget the chickens. Even though they started their lives together, one of them was growing and maturing faster than the other. Soon one of the boys became more like an older brother looking out for the younger one. After a few scoldings one was learning to mind the adults while the other continued to be slower to catch on.

The mother was still wary of what they did to the chicken and she was more vigilant in checking what they were up to. The boys started hunting for insects and bugs instead. That soon became the favourite outdoor pastime. The pond was full of frogs that they would catch and the barn still had a few mice that had escaped the cats. Then there were the puddles after a rain, the deeper the better. Scotty and

Freddy would splash until they were covered in mud from head to toe. It was great fun until the mother caught them. She yelled at them again and Freddy clearly understood that this was bad. Scotty not so much. He knew at the time but later seemed to forget all about it. Either that or he just could not resist the temptation to see how much water he could send flying through the air. Every wet day became a challenge for Freddy to try and stop Scotty from getting them into trouble.

Freddy did not like it when their mother was angry, he wanted to please her. Scotty on the other hand was more interested in his own wants and needs. There were many and it was difficult to keep him happy. One minute he was in the house, the next crying to go outside, then back in again. He wanted to explore everything, all the cupboards in the house, any hole in the ground, the homes of each creature's nest, roost, stall or pen. He was there looking at what was going on, making a disturbance and upsetting the peace of the farm. He kept mother, father and Freddy busy tending to his needs, feeding him, cleaning up after him and protecting him from trouble that would get him hurt. Freddy could not fathom why his buddy had grown to be so difficult. All Freddy needed was his food, a chance to explore the outdoors, get some exercise and come home to a warm bed.

This particular day was a little different. After breakfast Freddy and Scotty headed outside as usual.

It was a cold spring day. The ground had thawed and gone soft and mucky. New shoots of this year's crocuses had started to emerge but were covered in a thin layer of snow from the night before. That is when both boys noticed tracks in the snow. The animals had begun to move around more and the snow revealed the early morning activities of the wild ones. There were squirrel prints, trails from mice dragging their tails in the snow. There were large double footed hop marks from the local rabbits. There were lots of small birds scratching for seeds. Freddy and Scotty followed every track. Then they saw how some ended abruptly in a flurry of paw prints and talon marks from a large bird. In those places they could see that a hawk or eagle had attacked from above and taken them as prey.

In the spring, the air smelled fresh and clean and the earth seemed more exciting as it came alive again. Freddy and Scotty were just learning this and enjoying every moment. Some of the farm residents were expanding their families. New babies were bleating, chirping, mewing or whining incessantly at their mothers. Every pen, stall, roost and nesting area was bursting with activity. While some of the rescues had been returned to the wild, the numbers only seemed to increase as new creatures came to live at the farm. Freddy and Scotty were particularly interested in the barn owl with an injured wing. The vet had come to examine it and placed it in a temporary bandage. There were also some new raccoons that had been relocated, a litter of fox pups in need of support and one very rambunctious wolf pup that captured the boy's attention.

However all the newcomers took a back seat to this day in the wild. There were all sorts of new sights and smells that drew the boys towards a great adventure. Today they found some very large prints that wandered into the farm and made a mess of garbage strewn all over the ground. The smells and colours of all the food scraps had attracted a lot of attention. Mother and father were excitedly talking and making angry sounds as they tried to clean up and put things straight. There was much discussion and argument about fasteners and closures and building a shed for the garbage bins. Freddy and Scotty were more interested in what had done this and where they had gone. So while the parents were distracted, Scotty took off down the lane in pursuit of the unknown intruder. Freddy knew they were not allowed to travel beyond the big gate but Scotty disobeyed the rules.

Freddy had no option. He ran down the lane and out the gate to catch up with Scotty. He followed his tracks that led out the lane and down the road to the brook. He found Scotty at the water's edge wholly absorbed in catching the tadpoles. He was thoroughly enjoying himself and forgot that he was there to see who the big paw prints belonged to. Freddy just sat nearby and watched like a good friend does and Scotty as always was happy to have his company.

However the brook was running a little fast and high and on top of that Freddy saw who the big intruder was. There was a mother bear just on the other side of the brook watching Scotty and himself as one cub played nearby. Freddy pointed the bear out to Scotty who was curiously watching back. Freddy urged Scotty to come with him back home. It was really not safe and they were not allowed to be that far anyway. Scotty was stubborn and would not come so Freddy ran back home. He tried getting the attention of their mother and father but they just told him to go play. He pulled at their clothing to get their attention but they became irritated with him. They told him that they could not deal with him right now.

Freddy would not give up however and grabbed the papers their father had been reading and ran off out the door. Father was angry and chased Freddy all the way to the brook. The father spotted Scotty, now waist high in the water laughing and splashing and making gestures to try and spook the bear. Mother bears were often not feeling playful when they had a cub in tow but Scotty had no idea what he was getting into. Father rushed into the water and picked up Scotty and without saying a word, marched him directly home. Freddy followed along, still holding father's important papers. Once out of sight of the bear, father sternly told Scotty that he was in big trouble and told him that mama bears are notoriously cranky, fast and strong and she would not hesitate to protect her baby.

Then he looked at Freddy. His anger towards him had softened and he bent over and patted him gently. He said "thank you Freddy for being such a good friend, it is not everyday that someone is saved when a wolf cries boy". Then he scratched Freddy behind the ears and let him sleep in his favourite bed next to the stove with a fresh bone to chew on. Freddy was just happy to be home and that the day's adventures had ended well. Freddy knew that wolves grew up much faster than humans and he was OK with that. He knew Scotty would catch up eventually and that they would always remain best friends and brothers.

3 ENOUGH

When Leslie was three, she was always comparing herself to her bigger sister who was five at the time. Whatever Susan had, Leslie had to have, in the same way and the same amount. Looking back at an old photograph of the two of them eating their lunch at the outdoor picnic table, Leslie was eyeing her sister's sandwich, frowning and coveting something she thought was bigger and better tasting than her own. The competition between the two was fierce and followed them throughout their teenage years and beyond. Now that Leslie was in her fifties, she could see the destructive patterns in her life had begun a long time ago. Unfortunately it took five decades to unravel the events that lead her to the situation she now found herself in. This was never something she could ever believe would happen to her.

Leslie was a bright and pretty child, full of confidence and rebellious even in the early years. While some young people waited until their teenage years to challenge their parents and try to establish themselves as adults, Leslie did not wait and wanted to take everything life had to offer. Luckily her parents were relatively well off for a middle class family. Her father worked for the railway for as long as she could remember and her mother stayed home until the girls were in school. She then picked up a position as a secretary for a local insurance company. Since there were only two children, there was enough to go around with some extras that came from her mother's additional income. They had a nice big house in comparison to the others on the street. Their neighbours were mostly Catholics and they had bigger families with less resources to go around.

Both sisters were considered spoiled and entitled by the other children in the area. In some ways they were. Her mother never let them be seen in shabby play clothes and she always insisted that their father trade in the car as soon as a newer model came out. It was important to her that people thought they were well off. She always told the girls that you will be treated with more respect if you dress to command it. So that was how it was growing up as a bigger fish in a small pond. Leslie was an average student because her social life was busy and she was involved with the swim team, jazz dance, and played the flute in the school band. When she was finally able to get accepted at a local university, her parents were relieved. They wanted the girls to be well educated. Susan had always aspired to get a degree but not Leslie. Leslie went reluctantly and expected her parents to pay for it and they did.

There was an expectation for the sisters to find a good man and marry up in life. Leslie never questioned it. She had high standards, felt deserving and always got what she wanted. Her mother had always focused on her looks whether she gained or lost weight or how her hair colour suited her or not. It was ingrained in her to always look her best. She had a number of boy friends but none she considered serious long term relationship material. She wanted someone with money and prospects for a good career. Susan on the other hand did not cave in to the pressures of her parents and community and did not even take notice or realize what was expected of her. That often landed her in trouble with others but she had decided early on she wanted to go into farming and was always experimenting in the family garden. Susan was always happy with her lot in life and was content with whatever her parents provided.

Susan went to university to learn better horticulture practices. Leslie went to meet an interesting diversity of new people so she could travel in new social circles. Leslie never knew what it was like to not have life go her way. After she graduated with an Arts degree she had planned to get a teaching diploma. However she met Scott, who ticked off all the boxes she was seeking. He was tall and blond with unusually dark eyebrows. Scott had plans and wanted to settle down near his parents home and become more involved in the family hardware business. Scott was self assured, successful and wanted to marry Leslie. The small town however, was nowhere near a teacher's college. For the first time Leslie did not get her own way and compromised furthering her education so she could marry Scott. He was poised to take on a leadership role in a successful growing business.

The wedding was beautiful just as her parents had wanted for her. She and Scott had their home designed and constructed with a large wrap around deck. It had two stories with a deck off the top floor master bedroom. The view was scenic with rolling pastures and treed hills. Leslie and Scott raised one child who was born a year after their marriage. She never had the opportunity to teach and it was not until their son Andrew went to school that Leslie took up a volunteer position to help out at lunch. Leslie and Scott had money for whatever she wanted. When neighbours got something new Lessie had to one up them somehow. Her emotional feelings of contentment were tied to her perception that she had the best of everything. However she was easily unbalanced around people whom she thought had more money and who travelled. She was jealous of the exciting lifestyles of others. When she was unhappy, her fix was to go shopping.

Those riches would not last forever. Highwood Hardware took a risk on a very large international project that did not turn out well. Scott had to borrow to keep the business moving forward. For Leslie this was a very dark time. She was being held to a strict spending budget and was increasingly more depressed and angry with Scott for the position they were in. The couple could no longer host the large parties they once had and their friends started to dwindle. Andrew had to withdraw from private school and was having difficulty adjusting and making new friends. Scott became more preoccupied with the business. Andrew was getting older and not spending as much time with his mother, as expected. Leslie, with no work, no outlet for a bigger social life in such a small town, was increasingly lonely and miserable.

It seemed to Leslie that life was unfair. She did everything right and followed the plan for a happy life. By most people's standards she was fortunate to not be forced to work and had all the things many others coveted. She had a large beautiful home, new sport utility vehicle, expensive clothes, time and money for spas. Andrew was anxious to be on his own. He moved away from what was becoming a powder keg and took up law. Now Leslie had all the time in the world to herself to do whatever she pleased, if only she knew what that was. The dream of being a teacher was long gone. Her desire for more to fill that void created tension in the marriage. The money, the gifts and everything she had and was, including, Scott was not enough for her. When she didn't get what she wanted she withdrew from Scott. She did not do it intentionally to punish him but was just too foul tempered to be around. It did however push him so far away that Scott found someone else. While Andrew finished up at school and took on a new articling position on the other side of the country, Leslie was presented with divorce papers.

It was not like she did not see it coming but was shocked just the same. Scott had control over the money, had company lawyers to draw on and she went into the marriage with nothing. She was forced out into a small house on the other side of town and was expected to become employed before her support was reduced. Leslie was educated and had completed an arts degree at university. The expectation from the courts was that she could support herself. However Leslie did not know how to do that. Other than volunteering on occasion and managing her household, she had never been employed. She went from being cared for by her parents, directly to being kept by a husband. At age 50, Leslie found herself alone and owning very little. Her fair weather friends who hung around because of who she was married to and what she had, quickly disappeared. She was forced to mingle with people who she considered poor. Then because she was too proud to get a job she felt was beneath her, she plunged quickly from having enough money to buy anything she wanted to having barely enough to get by.

Susan and Leslie had drifted apart over the years. Susan was still single and living on her hobby farm near a small town over an hour away from their parents place. They did see each other on holidays when the entire family would congregate for Christmas and Easter. This Easter, Scott and her son Andrew would not be coming for the first time. It was always a busy time and the men always dominated the conversation with their stories and adventures about work and school. Leslie and Susan were always busy helping with the serving and cleaning up. This year it was quiet and after the meal had been settled, Susan asked Leslie if she wanted to join her on a walk. Leslie could not remember the last time she wandered the paths of their old acreage that took them across the brook, blueberry fields and over the hilly pasture to the pond. As they walked, childhood memories of peace and happiness began to flood Leslie's soul with the familiar feelings like the return of an old friend.

Susan was always quiet and kept her thoughts private. When they got to the pond they found the old camp where they used to spend hours as children. They sat on the stumps near the doorway facing the water as bees swarmed the wildflowers and the breeze fluttered the leaves of the aspen trees. It was quiet and serene. The apple tree beside the camp had grown very large but Leslie could still see the carving in the trunk, "sisters forever". Susan saw the carving and asked Leslie if she could remember the pledge they had made. Leslie had forgotten but as Susan spoke she began to remember how they promised each other that no matter what happened in their future lives, they would always have each other. Leslie asked Susan how she could stand being alone on that farm of her all these years. Susan said she was never alone as long as she knew she had her family and her sister, if not nearby but in her heart and thoughts. Susan said that her life had been blessed to have family and a safe place to live and she reminded herself every day how lucky she was.

Leslie felt her heart stir back to a time when she had believed that too. Her life had been a rat race to grow up, succeed, live up to the expectations of others and play out a prescribed "formula" that would shower her with joy and happiness. She diligently followed the program of good grades, education, good husband, nice house and lots of money but it failed her. She constantly worried about what others thought of her. All her wants and desires urged her to constantly look at her cup as half empty. That feeling of never having enough stemmed from her feelings that she was not enough. That dissatisfaction spilled over into her marriage and landed her in a place where she had to start over. Leslie had lost what happiness felt like and did not know where to find it. Now as she felt the warmth of the sun and looked upon her childhood haven, she remembered.

The joy was in the being, not doing. It was in the gratitude, not the getting. Her original, unjaded child like self was hiding quietly in her heart waiting for her to return. It took fifty years to realize that she always had everything she needed. She had forgotten and had lost her balance. She realized with the help of a loving sister that she was someone who was beautiful, important, special and that she always was enough. The next stage of Leslie's new life would be different because she had finally returned home to herself.

4 Iniquity or Inequity?

The high school English teacher, Miss Clarke sometimes confused words like iniquity and inequity. The only difference is the "i" is replaced with an "e". She of course knew better but did it to see who was paying attention, waiting for someone to correct her. Some of the class would just chuckle quietly because they knew what she was doing but wanted to see who else would catch on. Rebekah was the best student in the class and she would glance over with a smirk at her best buddies Ross and Katie. They would then respond with a nod looking back towards the five students who everyone knew were slower than most. They of course did not notice. Then the teacher wrote the two words on the blackboard and asked one of the "five" to tell her which word she should have used.

Not many schools included curriculum for vocabulary or had Spelling Bees anymore. However this private school was a stickler for improving the use of language. The school even kept Latin, decades after every other public school had dropped it. This school expected their graduates to excel in the sciences as well as the arts. Latin being the base of much of scientific nomenclature, was therefore considered required. Every student was also expected to master a second language, take instruction in religion and participate in debates, fund their own travel excursions to other countries, attend social outreach programs and volunteer in the community. Their alumni were known for taking on leadership roles in the community and around the globe.

It took a great deal of money to pay for a spot in this institution. The same wealthy families who came from the affluent neighbourhoods, the doctors, lawyers, politicians and those with cushy government jobs, always sent their children here as a rite of passage. Even though there were entrance exams, their children were guaranteed a position because of who they were. The school tried to hide this bias and was in fact found to be deficient in an audit for accreditation. The school lacked diversity in the student population and even though some of the teachers were aware of the issue, they did not dare voice their concerns. The school was nudged into offering scholarships to lower income but promising candidates from the surrounding public schools.

Shelley was one of these students. She was

one of the brightest in her junior high and her parents wanted her to have the best education. They lived in a row of townhouses near the industrial area of town. Both her parents worked, her dad in construction and her mom at a bank. She had three younger siblings and there was no way that Shelley would have had the opportunity to attend this private school without the scholarship. With the support of her parents, she applied and was accepted. Shelley was grateful for the opportunity and worked hard to keep her grades as high as she could so she could continue there. If her grades fell below even a high average, she could lose the spot.

Shelley was one of Miss Clarke's favourites and Shelly was aware that this dynamic was not taken lightly by other students. Her education was not only academic in nature but she observed the social interactions and hierarchies at play. The "five" were looked down upon by the smart students but were not singled out in any obvious way. Their aloofness was carefully masked and reduced to nods and grins among trusted friends. These five were some of the students who would never pass the strict entrance exams but whose influential families pushed them to be there. They were the trouble makers that flaunted their privilege in the teachers' faces, daring them to fail them. The five did not want to be there and made life miserable for the others.

In particular they did not like Shelley and

behind her back called her the "welfare student". Shelley was also disliked by the wealthy smart kids who felt they deserved more of the teacher's attention than she. Every time she put up her hand and tried to participate in class, if the teacher engaged her, she would see the others rolling their eyes, making faces or squinting at each other. They were not obvious about it and Shelley was not sure if the teacher ever noticed, but Shelley did. Rebekah, Ross and Katie ran the social circles. They were not only rich and smart but they were the most popular. They had study groups and ran extracurricular events. They decided who got the invites to whatever was going on and everyone wanted to be on their list. Almost everyone was on that list who was of the same race and culture. Even the "five" were on that list but not Shelley and not students who were non-white or non-English speaking.

Shelley did not care about not being invited to events with people she did not really care for. However, the other students made it difficult for her to succeed. Some of the expectations of the school required her to spend money she didn't have. The popular kids had groups set up for fundraising for international travel trips but always forgot to inform Shelley of the meetings. Shelly had to fund-raise on her own, going door to door in her own neighbourhood, selling baked goods at the local market and hustling local businesses. Then when volunteer lists were put up for social outreach, the lists were always full before she found out about them. The uniforms were important to be kept clean and tidy and the families had to purchase them. Shelly had only two outfits that she rotated. Twice she had to replace her shirt and skirt when someone accidentally spilled ink on them.

The shirts were white and long sleeved, except in the warmer months. Shelley always wore long sleeved shirts. The skirts were black, navy and green plaid, pleated and could not be more than one inch above the knee. The knee socks could be black or navy blue but the oxford shoes always had to be black. They all had matching plaid vests with the school crest but that was optional. Many had a collection of vests. Shelley only owned the single one she was required to buy, but did not wear it unless it was mandatory for a special convocation ceremony. They could not wear makeup or jewellery and their hair, if longer than shoulder length, had to be pinned up. Many of the girls would hike up the skirts when the teachers were not around, wear large earrings and put on makeup on breaks or while off school property. It was a competition to see who was the coolest and see how far they could go before they were caught.

When on a school outing, it was imperative that they act and dress in a way that honoured the reputation of the school. Most were good at doing that, even the rebellious students. That was something that would get them trouble not just with the school but their parents. There was a competition for everything including the best extracurricular activities. Visiting the children's hospital was valued above visiting the seniors home. Working on the community newspaper and organizing drives to collect food and clothing for those in need, was far higher on everyone's list than feeding the homeless at the local soup kitchen or sorting clothes for the second hand shops. The latter two activities were the ones Shelley always ended up doing. Some of the classmates that accompanied her would signal to her and make faces as they worked, making fun of the people they were supposed to help. However Shelley did not mind and started to look forward to seeing her new found friends.

One afternoon, when the students were transported to their various outreach work locations, Shelley was accompanied by Rebekah, Ross and Katie to the soup kitchen. It seems the three were caught smoking behind the school and were sent for the next three weeks to work alongside Shelley as punishment. Neither Shelley nor her three classmates were happy about the situation. When they arrived the three new workers seemed nervous and giggled. They had no idea what to do, so they looked to Shelley to show them the ropes. They did what they were told but they would not interact with the homeless, just look at them with blank expressions that reminded Shelley of a mixture of fear and shock. They were speechless when Shelly addressed some of the visitors in a friendly, familiar way, even asking about their families and how they were making out on specific challenges.

Afterwards, the three newbies asked Shelley how she managed to work there and why she would stoop to speaking to them? Shelley realized that her classmates had been so thoroughly insulated in their own social bubble, they could not relate. They said that these homeless people would not be there if they had jobs, refrained from getting addicted to drugs and took responsibility for themselves. Shelley explained how some, through no fault of their own, had experienced personal tragedies that affected their mental health, how some could not afford the drugs they needed, while others were trying to get a job. Not having a stable home and access to clean clothes and bathing facilities, was making that leap to employment difficult. Some people had escaped their homes because of abusive situations and that being homeless was the preferred choice. She told them that most people do not choose to be homeless and nobody makes it a part of their long-term plan.

The next day Shelley expected the trio to make fun of her at school for supporting the homeless but they didn't mention it. They were a little friendlier to her and she felt she had earned a little bit of respect. The others however teased Rebekah, Ross and Katie for having to work at the soup kitchen. They made all sorts of disparaging remarks about homeless people and made the trio out to be bleeding hearts that would give handouts to anyone. Some of the seniors even came up to Ross and faked a need for food and money to try and make him angry. Ross tried to tell them they didn't know anything about being homeless and that they should try it sometime and see how they liked it. They just laughed at him. Miss Clarke and other teachers were aware of what was happening but did not intervene.

That afternoon was when Miss Clarke chose to obfuscate the words "iniquity" and "inequity". After writing the words on the board, and getting no response from the five who she noted were not paying attention, she turned the question to the rest of the class. Rebekah said that "iniquity" was an evil deed or sin. Then Katie responded that "inequity" was something that was not fair or equal. Miss Clarke asked the class if they thought Katie and Rebekah were correct. Everyone agreed. Then the teacher asked "how many of you would say that these two words are very different and have no similarities to each other". Again most students agreed but not all of them. A few members of the class said that in some ways they were similar. This was surprising to most who just looked at the surface of the meanings.

Miss Clarke was curious what the dissenters thought and asked them to explain. One student said that inequity and inequality was unfair and in some cases, taken to the extreme, could cause some people to have everything and others nothing. If this was food for example, then the inequity would constitute a moral crime and would become an iniquity. Another student agreed but added that this happens all the time in more moderate ways when CEOs get huge salaries and their employees get much lower wages so that all the company benefits only the few. The unfairness upsets morale at companies, unions come in, people go on strike and the resulting antagonistic environment affects people not just financially but emotionally. This would become an iniquity as well.

The class started thinking about the similarities and talking among themselves as they came up with new scenarios. Miss Clarke asked the class to refocus for a minute and see if they could come up with any examples that were closer to home or from their own experiences. Rebekah spoke up about the hidden hierarchy within the school. Some students felt they were smarter and more privileged than others and put others down or unfairly judged them. That inequity in their own school population affected how some students performed better than others, by affecting how some individuals felt about themselves. Therefore it was iniquity in the way students were unfairly judged and treated by others, when some were not supported and encouraged to do their best but in fact were discouraged from doing so.

Miss Clarke wanted to know what Shelley thought given she was at the school on scholarship.

Shelley spoke carefully and reflected on her own treatment at the school. She told them how she struggled to succeed because of the barriers placed in her way just because her family was not as affluent as others at this school. She told them how hard she worked to just keep up, the financial burdens she felt that went unnoticed by others and how much she valued her education there. She said the bigger inequity was that other students like her were unable to experience the higher quality of education that she was now privileged to be a part of. The greater iniquities are that some well deserving students would miss opportunities in life because of the inequity while those who did have the greater opportunities were not grateful and squandered their education. Miss Clarke smiled at her and looked at the class knowingly and said, "Well said Shelley. I agree". For homework, she told the class to do a personal inventory of things to be grateful for and with that fitting end, dismissed the class for the day.

5 Jerusalem Hill

The small mountain overshadowing Bryn Lake had always been there since the glaciers carved out the landscape. When the ice retreated, it scattered the earth with massive grey boulders, studded with glittering pink and white feldspar. Then melting waters flooded the land to form lakes and streams. Early vegetation consisted of hearty moss, clover, blueberry, coltsfoot, and horsetail. The white umbels topping the yarrow and pearly everlasting came later, followed by the yellow bolts of hawk-weed, dandelion and goldenrod. Over time these created enough vegetable matter, to form a soil habitable for the raspberry, blackberry, wild rose, honeysuckle, pussy willow and alder. Finally scraggy black spruce shot tall into the sky between the rocks, grasping whatever earth its predecessors left behind. All this time, the mountain was a witness to this blossoming of life over the eons of time.

It was the late 60's when Shaunna first discovered Bryn Lake. It was here, where her parents bought a large piece of land, on a cove facing the small but significant mountain. The property had been cleared of most of the trees except one maple with a long bare trunk thirty feet high and a burst of bent branches at the top, reaching out in the four directions of the earth. The remaining evergreens, white and yellow birch and aspen, lined ditches along the borders. The notable exception was a rowan tree, facing the northern edge near the water. There was a fire pit near the shoreline, a dug well midway up the slope and a patch of trees in the south, at the top of the property along the subdivision's access road. The entire property mostly consisted of rock, thinly veiled in barren soil, with granite and shale reaching deep into the bedrock. This stony vista extended around the shoreline and into the water.

Shaunna's father spent every moment he could, developing the property. The land provided a good supply of stone for a fireplace and the footing of a dock. A small cottage was constructed. The bare ground was raked free of the larger rocks while grass seeds were hopefully sown. The grass that survived, learned to share the space with the wild things in what became more of a meadow than a lawn. Small feathery, long needled white pine, were transplanted to the bare southwestern slope to create a privacy barrier. After a few attempts to construct driveways, the flattened area at the top of the southwestern elevation, became home to a parking area. This was the backdrop for the abode known as Bryn Awel (Hill Breeze), tucked into the slope of the hill, facing the wind and water of Bryn Lake, with a view of the omnipresent mountain.

When Shaunna was a child she dreamt she could fly, saw visions of skies from the surface of other planets and remembered being a druid elder, even though she did not know what that was at the time. Like most children, she believed in magic, fairies and otherworldly creatures. Shaunna was good at whatever she tried to master, whether it was ballet or academics. She knew she could excel at any career and that every opportunity was available to her. The busyness with goals, ambitions and achievements satisfied her for a time, until she noticed that something was missing. She thought back to the carefree days of her childhood, laying in the grass with her pet turtle, excited by the little plants, the clover and crawling bugs, while filled with amazement and curiosity. Shaunna realized that she had grown up and had forgotten the magic of her youth.

It was in her early twenties, when that emptiness set in. She began a search to recapture that missing element of wonder and joy. It was that persistent, underlying motivation that drove her to travel the world seeking out special places, believed to hold magical powers. In particular she travelled to

Wales, Britain, France and Arizona, to study castles, mazes, ancient stone circles and energy vortexes. She was especially drawn to Stonehenge and Avebury and experienced unusual energy fields while there. Through the years of education, careers, marriage and child rearing, Shaunna held the wonders of what she had experienced in her heart. She kept an inventory of her miraculous encounters and answers to prayers, alive in her memory. For Shaunna, all her wanderings made sense, in the big picture of her life purpose.

It was in these later years that she returned to Bryn Awel to continue with what her father had begun. Just as Shaunna had matured, Bryn Awel had evolved and changed. The white pine had grown to over seventy feet tall. The birch had aged and some were dying. The trees had spread their branches over the property making it a shady, but happy, place for the hostas and ferns surrounding the cottage. Wild flowers of all types and cultivated roses, filled the air with colours and aromas. Familiar creatures with their joyful chattering, happy chirps, songs and buzzing, formed a choir with the melodious tinkling and gongs of the wind chimes. At night twinkle lights danced in the trees, mirroring the dark starry sky. The cottage doubled in size and a garage with an extended parking area, was constructed on the terraced southwestern slope.

On the surface, Bryn Awel looked like any other lakefront property in the area. To most, it was a valuable piece of real estate. It is like every wild place that remains unknown to people who are detached from the natural world, in that it is viewed as just a material asset. To Shaunna however, it was her home, a place her father loved and where she and her family shared happy memories. Only someone like Shaunna, would notice the strange subtleties that made Bryn Awel different from any other acreage. The lake itself was remarkably deep at forty feet, just ten feet from the shoreline. At the outer edge of her cove, where a point of blue shale outcroppings extended into the middle of the lake, there was a pit so deep, it was deemed bottomless. Then there was the large, unidentified lake creature, believed to have come up stream from the ocean, where it became trapped, after the floods of the 70's.

Sitting just above the fire pit, at the water's edge, was the giant flat rock, unearthed during a renovation. It was three feet high and approximately fifteen square feet on the upper surface. It had a notch on the side that served as a step. The first time Shaunna stood on it she had a vision that she was a Druid priest, delivering a homily. It harkened her back to similar dreams she had as a child. She felt a heightened calmness when near the water and on her rock by the fire pit. For Shaunna, that spot inspired her to pray, as if contact with the divine, was magnified at that particular location. Shaunna learned to see the miraculous in the common. As she did, Bryn Awel began to reveal itself as an extraordinary place. The big flat rock became her holy altar, where worries were unloaded, healing was manifested and she could co-created her future, with inspired prayer, forged in gratitude.

Slowly Shaunna began to recognize a peculiar feel of energy that reminded her of the exceptional places from her travels. There was something unique about her property. When Shaunna used high frequency tuning forks to cleanse the air, the vibrations would disappear at the granite property markers, as if they had absorbed or synchronized with the energy of the stones. At certain angles, the crooked limbs in the upper canopy, that crowned the lone bare maple trunk, formed the shape of a heart. An indigenous shaman meditating near this tree, reported how a selenite column of crystal jumped out of her pouch and landed at the base of this tree. She claimed this was a tree of life and that the crystal should remain there undisturbed. For the initiated, such a tree was a portal to the underworld, middle earth and heavens, where the spirits could communicate with us.

From an aerial view, Bryn Lake was shaped like a crucifix. Shanna's patch of land was located in a cove on the western arm, at the head of the cross. Despite the existence of the alleged sea-monster, Shaunna loved to swim in the cold, clear, clean, refreshing water. Her favourite place was the white sand beach, at the far northern end of the lake, at the foot of the cross. It was fed by three streams from the mountain at the eastern end of the beach. When sitting on the beach facing south on a calm and sunny day, the shallow water would shimmer with vibrant brilliance. Three communication towers at the top of the mountain, reminded Shaunna of the three crosses, at Christ's Crucifixion. Shaunna was amazed to discover that the sparkles were created by gold tailings from an old mine. Her mountain that supplied these riches both materially and symbolically, was called Jerusalem Hill.

Shaunna wondered if sacred places become that way, when loving, kind and caring people, regularly gather in that particular space. Is it possible for such good energy to be absorbed and accumulated into the memories of the rocks and trees, where it can echo into a future time? Then again, she wondered if she herself had a particular gift, that could endow any place she called home, with magic, because of her acknowledgement and gratitude for nature's gifts. Deep down she knew that all places on earth could be considered supernatural, for those that learn how to connect with its secrets. Holy places emerge from the web connecting land, people, good intentions and unseen forces. The sacred union of man and nature, can release providential encounters and blessings, anyplace in the world. The magic element lies in its embrace.

Shaunna believed Bryn Awel had a lot in

common with the holy and sacred places she had visited around the world. Bryn Awel embodied a similar spiralling of benevolent energy and sense of goodness and peace. Underground springs, believed to make Stonehenge and Lourdes places of miracles, also existed in the same way, under Bryn Awel. The stone formations of blue rock and feldspar filled granite rock, were also common features with the stone composition on her property. The gracious blessings received by many at Bryn Awel, were beautiful outcomes and evidence that, like some famous holy sites of pilgrimages, Bryn Awel too was graced with divine influences. The crooked maple was most likely a marker for a sacred place, known by the indigenous people. Shaunna concluded that long ago, someone other than herself, knew the area was holy, when they named the mountain Jerusalem (Place of Peace) Hill.

For Bryn Awel, the twinkling night-time illuminations, the joyful tweets, diverse greenery, intoxicating aromas and rustling of aspen leaves, was an outward cloak of beauty that belied the secrets of a miraculous potential. Even if all this was known to the earliest inhabitants, it would remain a mystery in Shaunna's lifetime. The birch and other hardwood trees would continue to grow until they succumbed to old age, powerful winds or destructive storms. Rains would erode the soil, flatten hills, fill valleys and wash the earth away to the sea. Such changes would hardly be noticed by Shaunna's descendants. However the old maple and her offspring, would continue as the watchers and rememberers. Long after collective memories had faded, Jerusalem Hill would remain a guardian of Bryn Awel and a witness to its magnificence.

6 Just Saying

It was nearing the end of the last semester and the deadline for applications for a coveted spot at the Emma Brown School of Design was fast approaching. Both Emily and Samantha (Sam) wanted to be accepted. They were just two of fifteen classmates, who had come to the local art college as a preparatory year for the prestigious school. The students had been working all year to create material for their portfolios which included not just samples of their work, but needed to showcase creativity, with a variety of mediums and styles. The portfolios had to be visually striking, well organized and cleverly presented if they hoped to be accepted. There were very few spots available and good academic grades, as well as the ability to communicate passion and desire, were also factored into the eligibility requirements.

The class was tightly knit and they had all

become good friends over the past year. The classmates were supportive of one another. If someone missed a class, students like Sam, would provide them with a copy of their notes. After touring the campus they got together to discuss their insights as to what they thought the school might be looking for. They encouraged one another about how they could do just as well, or better, than the current students based on the artworks they saw. However as the deadline loomed closer and competition heightened, the relationships became frayed. The entire milieu had shifted. In addition to the backhanded compliments to shake the confidence of their classmates, they had intentional confusion added to the mix to disrupt productivity. As tensions mounted, Emily and others had started using "trash talk" to intimidate and demoralize those they now viewed as "opponents".

Their teachers instructed them to prepare 20 original pieces, but now some of the students disputed that. One announced, *"I just wanted to let you guys know, a friend of mine at the design school, heard that this year, the committee was looking for at least 25 pieces, with a sample of abstract acrylic and modern sculpture...just saying"*.

Emily, not to be outdone replied in a bored tone, *"Meh, I had heard that too. But I heard they are also looking specifically for someone who can do lithograph sketching and screen printing. Those classes have been shrinking and they are looking to boost those classes ...just saying."* Now everyone was confused and angry that they had not been told about this new information. That was going to put many of them behind schedule. Those who did not use the specific mediums mentioned, felt extremely discouraged.

Some of the class felt they had been misled and were now at a huge disadvantage. Others accused Emily and the other students of making up stories just to confuse everyone. One skeptic, seeing through the game being played, sarcastically responded, *"I heard, the sculptures must be at least three feet high and gold plated...just saying!"*. Now, each student needs to run for their lives, it is survival of the fittest, each artist for themself.

Emily had been particularly hard on one of the students. She was rattled and asked Sam for her opinion. Sam took a look at the watercolour and asked her some questions. The landscape was a scene from her grandparents farm that meant a lot to her. She had used a different technique on the barn because that was the feature she wanted to highlight. Sam told her, *"It is a lovely view and the barn does stand out. I can see you put your heart into this. That is what counts"*.

Emily was the class favourite, with her trendy clothes and confidence. She led the social network, planned the events and always had something to say about somebody. Sam and Emily had been friends but that would soon end. *"Love the colours you chose for that piece, too bad the perspective is off a bit. Good job just the same. I can help you get it right, I'm here if you need me... just saying"*, said Emily to Sam, with fake concern. Sam knew what Emily was trying to do, so she doubled down on her concentration. Just when everyone needed to be organized, the "trash talk" had students second guessing themselves. "Just saying", was a cover-up, to hide the real intent, as if the words spoken were just an afterthought, with no particular importance. The phrase was like closing the pen after all the chickens had already escaped.

Even Sam was questioning her approach. She tried to brush it off but she was angry. She could not believe Emily and some of the others could be so cruel and calloused, to purposely use words to be mean and obstructive towards others and their work. Sam learned a long time ago about the impact words could have on a person's life. Sam's father almost prevented her from seeking a career in art. He called her works of art, "the childish preoccupation of someone who refuses to grow up". Sam did not allow her father to discourage her. Neither was she going to let the now toxic classroom, full of negative judgment, criticism and misinformation, become a roadblock for her. Sam had already been established as the class oddball. She was quiet, wore jeans and T-shirts, with sneakers and a hoodie. She did not wear makeup, was pretty but plain and always tried to choose her words carefully.

Sam did not have time to party and socialize. She was behind in her projects because she needed money and worked part-time, at the local second-hand thrift shop. In Sam's job as a cashier, she saw many people who were down on their luck. She made it her business to offer a kind word when she could. One older lady would come in early every Saturday morning, before the regular crowd. She was small, plump, with grey hair pulled up to an old fashioned top knot, that was neat and tidy. Sam supposed that she was on a low end fixed income like most customers. However she really did not know much except that she loved art like Sam did. When it was not busy, their conversation would gravitate towards how to better create a skyline with watercolour or techniques of layering colours in oil. Today she asked, *"how is school going?"*

Sam was still feeling a bit disorientated from lastclass's kerfuffle, and responded by saying, *"I am not so sure"*. She told the lady about the application deadline and her portfolio and how she was now questioning her plans. She had lost a bit of confidence and was not sure she would even be able to compete well in the running. Surprisingly, her elderly friend wanted more detail and encouraged her to focus on the pieces that meant the most to her emotionally.

She ensured that a few quality pieces with

heart, that would move others, would have far more impact than a larger quantity of technical pieces. Sam was not so sure that people would be able to tell the difference. Then the lady told her that well trained artists had an eye for passion and could always tell the difference. *"Good visual art, like good music, should be able to move someone to tears"*, she said.

The next class was just as stressful as the previous one. Some of her classmates started to panic. The argument about the best way forward with the portfolios continued. Sam stayed quiet and did not participate. She took her elderly friend's advice and started looking at the pieces that meant something to her. Instead of just checking off the technical boxes, she chose the pieces by how they made her feel. This helped her stay grounded and centred on her original plans, amidst the chaos of the class. Some of her classmates had formed camps of opinion and were heavily engaged in arguing their own perspectives when they eventually noticed Sam's silence. Slowly, one by one they started watching her. The room went quiet and Emily spoke up and said. *"Sam, what do you think?"*.

Sam knew that no matter what she said she would be roasted. *"I am not just saying...I believe that the committee will be looking for quality over technical quantity and that they should see our passion in the pieces we present. I believe this is what will decide whether we get in or not"*. Sam could see that some of the students were nodding in agreement with her.

Emily however was not convinced and responded, *"I guess we all have to come up with some rationale, to justify to ourselves, that less is more. Self-deception may make you feel better, but won't get you a spot at the design school,...just saying"*. Some of the students chuckled at Emily's words as they looked down their noses at those students they had already pre-judged to be at the bottom of the class.

Sam added, *"I am not just saying... but a customer I know from the store, who seems to know a lot about art, told me this and I believe her"*. Sam had immediately regretted what she said. Now even the students that had nodded in agreement were laughing at her.

Emily piped up, *"if you want to put your art career in the hands of a poor old lady who shops at a second-hand thrift store, you have already lost the competition as far as I am concerned. Sorry to be so harsh but someone has to say it. You might as well give up now and not waste anyone's time...just saying"*.

Sam was embarrassed and put her head down to pretend she was deep into her work. She thought to herself, *"maybe Emily is right, who am I trying to fool with my wishful thinking"*. However, while the other students were preparing their essays and rehearsing faux interview questions, to tell the committee about their passion for art, Sam continued instead by picking out pieces of work that she was passionate about.

Everyone believed the new information regarding portfolio requirements. So much so, they pressured the teachers to create extra curricular classes, for those who wanted to develop skills in lithography, screen printing and sculpture. The school set up mock interviews and the teachers were editing essays, to highlight these wider range of technical abilities. Sam was trying to stick to her original plan with a smaller range of the skills that she was most proficient with. In any case she had run out of time. She still had two pieces left to finish, one in pen and ink and the other a watercolour. Then she went back to some of her older pieces that inspired her to become an artist in the first place. She chose a scene that started with pencil and later finished in acrylic. It was a scene from a place she cherished next to a river, in an old apple orchard where she had vacationed with her family.

There was something about her art that she loved. It was not the final product but the process of creating it that made her feel connected to the world around her. The creative process was a sacred place that brought joy and excitement to her otherwise mundane world. Looking at the surroundings, through an artistic eye, one trained to see the finest details of light, colour, shapes and lines was like uncovering a treasure. The more she practised the better she got and greater were the secrets revealed to her. At one stage she practised water and sky lines until she found out how they merged with the shadows and clouds. For a long time faces were an enigma until she finally mastered how to represent what she was seeing. These were all exciting accomplishments for Sam. This journey in learning about art and her ability to see the details, would be the basis of her portfolio story.

After each student had submitted their portfolios, they waited for an admissions interview. Emily was one of the first to get a call back for an appointment. It had been 10 days before Sam had heard back. She had started to get worried. She was the last in her class but did get a time slot, the next morning on the last day of admittance. Emily was surprised telling her how lucky she was to squeak in at the very end, perhaps luck was on her side and someone cancelled. Sam was not going to let Emily's words discourage her. Sam's last name started with a "W" and the calls may have been arranged alphabetically. She chose to think that. Sam caught an early bus to make sure she was there on time. Along the entire bus route she daydreamed and envisioned herself as a student at the Emma Brown School of Design. Then the bell chimed for her stop, bringing her back to reality and the task at hand.

Sam found the main administration building, a

stately large grey stone structure, with a dome and massive clock at the top. There were three sets of concrete stairs with steel railings working their way up to a set of two large carved wooden doors. Students were sitting along the steps laughing and enjoying themselves. She just stared straight ahead, intent on finding the correct location. She was relieved that when she stepped into the vaulted ceiling entrance there was clear signage leading to the interview room. She was told she would be questioned by a dozen seasoned artists that made up the committee. Sam was prepared to expect that. She was curious about her portfolio and was surprised that the boardroom was empty of people and all her pieces of art had been mounted on the walls.

Slowly the committee members entered the room. They were talking among themselves and examining her pieces of art. One man introduced himself to her as an artist in residence for the provincial art gallery. He said he liked the watercolour of the apple orchard because it had a very peaceful serene feel about it. Then when the meeting began, Sam was asked to discuss each piece she had selected and why. She was able to explain the inspiration behind each piece and what it meant to her as an artist. Then part way through the interview Sam saw a familiar face. The chairperson's hair was grey and distinguished with a neat knot on top of her head and a kind face. Sam recognized the woman smiling at her. Today she was not wearing the thrift store clothes she had purchased at her store but a smart pantsuit and scarf.

Sam felt instantly reassured of the credibility of the advice she had taken. Those words enabled her to successfully showcase her creativity. It gave her the strength to ignore her father's expressed negative opinions of art and artists. It gave her the mindfulness to shield her from the hurtful comments, carelessly flung like daggers around the classroom by Emily and others. Those words are disguised as casual and harmless... "Just Saying", almost prevented her from finishing her portfolio. Sam experienced the power of words. The kind words she shared with others at the thrift store, had come back to bless her tenfold. If it had not been for her willingness to try and brighten the day of others she may not have been accepted to the Emma Brown School of Design. Sam was grateful for the opportunity and would always be thankful for the uplifting words shared with her by a kind lady, when she needed it most.

7 THE LIGHT KEEPER

It was a strangely beautiful place of isolation and starkness. The island was a half mile from a remote village on a barren north eastern coastline. This where Katie spent her formative years among barnacled rock awash with massive stalks of giant kelp. The bodies of which stretched along the high tide mark twisted around old bones of sun bleached driftwood and the aromatic stench of various other species of rotting seaweed. The government wharf had taken so many beatings, it was abandoned. The tiny grey pebbled beach nestled in the ubiquitous rock, was now the only place where Katie and her father, Sam, could safely launch the Zodiac for school or supplies.

The island's shoreline was a wavy line of sea-worn granite boulders of all shapes and sizes. The land mass was not flat and rose at an angle from sea level, as a one sided hill towards the east. On the highest point farthest from the mainland, was a monstrous blue-black shale outcropping reaching over two hundred feet into the sky. The foot of this cliff precariously stretched another several hundred feet out to sea. It was this finger of death, hidden beneath the crashing waves at mid and high tides, that had changed the course of many lives. Not only for the victims and families who lost loved ones, but also for the mainlanders who had witnessed the tragedies or were called upon to assist the ill fated.

It was at the apex of the ominous tower of rock, where the old red trimmed, whitish, salt stained lighthouse stood. Alongside this clutched the faded blue, hip roofed, wood framed family home. This solitary ten acre crop of rock, cloaked in a thin layer of soil, was also home to bogs, brooks and miniature spruce. The mercurial wind was ever present either whispering secret messages or shouting great proclamations. Calm days of repetitive lapping, popping and hiss of tiny bubbles was a soothing background ambience. Other times thunderous claps and airborne spray was an intrusion into one's very own thoughts. At night, overt orchestrations aroused the imagination of an angry Poseidon. Even when wind was not heaving ocean guts upon the rocks, screaming gulls were engaged in high frequency fights over a new corpus delicti served up by nature's food chain.

For those who did not know the island like Katie, it was a noisy, chaotic and desolate place. As a child who grew up there, she had learned to appreciate the cacophony of wondrous life cycling in corners, hidden from the untrained eye. The shore rocks cradled pools for starfish and crab. The thicket beside their house was home to families of robin and sparrow who returned every spring. The swallows had claimed the rafters of their barn, bald eagles had nested in trees and rocks along the cliffs, while frogs and peepers kept a chorus in the sheltered pond. Katie knew the location of every patch of mayflower and eagerly anticipated the emergence of the crocus, coltsfoot and pussy willow. Every inch of the island from the inland lupin, to shore dotted bayberry and cormorant fishing from the rocks, was home to something unique and beautiful.

The originally small family abode had grown in sections to become an eighteen hundred square foot patchwork residence. Most recently bulging after the insistence of Katie's mother for a newer, larger en-suite master bedroom and kitchen. Sam spared no expense to make his wife happy as he became more and more aware of her growing discontent. When Katie's mother left them, Sam took it upon himself to do the best he could. Katie, at only ten, tried to make the house comfortable and learned to cook, while they both tended to the grief of the situation. For Katie's sake Sam forged a closer connection to the community and rigorously involved himself in school matters. On the days too dangerous to venture off island, he would hold class on their modest kitchen table.

Sam was well respected for the role he had taken on in Katie's life despite the responsibility of tending the lighthouse. He and his father had always lived on the island. It was a job Sam did with a sense of duty to the fisher people of the town. The sea is a precarious place to make a living. Fish were still abundant on this little patch of coastline. Sam was deeply appreciated as a pragmatic person, quiet and awkward with small talk. When he did have something to say however, it was generally well thought out and delivered with conviction. No matter what the issue, Sam was a good listener and his presence at meetings had a calming effect. People would turn to his common sense to mediate the loud voices that tend to polarize and immobilize many small towns.

Katie worked hard in her academics and earned a scholarship for university. Her mother had left to pursue the education she had longed for. Her father, while disappointed, understood the worthiness of those dreams. Sam's mother also felt oppressed by the island. Sam had recognized the signs early on and knew he had to accept that. Not everyone could sustain the solitude of this particular lifestyle. For Katie however, it was a safe place, familiar and steadfast, where her father was always available and she was adored by canine friend, Jake. Her father had instilled in her a belief that whatever one did, must be done well. Sam also told Katie not to forget who she was and that she had special powers. He told her that their family had a secret and that she would always be a Light Keeper, no matter where life took her.

Katie's mother sent her a letter every month painting a world of exciting possibilities. Directly after high school graduation, Katie moved to study and reconnect with her mother. When she completed her biology degree, she applied to veterinary college with no success. She had good grades but not a lot of animal experience. She helped out at two vet clinics but the volunteers were fiercely competitive for the too few coveted recommendations, needed for a successful entrance application. Instead, Katie happened upon an outreach program at a clinic that supported lone-parent mothers that needed volunteers. She fell in love with helping the families and decided to take more courses to switch to community nursing. Soon she landed a position she was excited about, where she quickly became someone many grew to love and rely on for support.

As Katie became more involved with the families and the community she supported, her belief in health prevention grew. Access to stable housing, good food, clean water, a safe environment, affordable education, opportunity, social fairness and justice were necessary for physical, mental and emotional wellness. Her clients however were unable to reap these benefits because they were either working two jobs, overly stressed or too poor. Poverty was inevitable for many of her clients when even the institutions that were supposed to help, failed to collect child support or provide sufficient funding for basic needs. Society had let down those, on whose shoulders sat the hope of our next generation. Katie could not control the epigenetics affecting the health of her clients, but she could repair the outcomes. However this was not enough. Katie believed we had to do better.

When she returned home she would usually take two weeks of vacation. This time she took a break for a month and a half. A new nurse with excellent credentials has been recruited to the practice. She knew her people would be well cared for. Katie planned to use this opportunity to reacquaint herself with every nook and cranny of her island refuge. Upon arrival she was greeted by an overly excited Jake and said hello to all her plant and animal friends. She went to the bog to see the purple irises. The din of the peepers went silent upon her approach. She smiled to herself and waited quietly for the chorus to resume. She welcomed the gale force of sweet salt air in her face, cleansing her of the dirty remnants of the world she had come to escape. The mainland had lost the allure it had in her teenage years. She wondered why she had stayed away so long.

The island always helped her to return to work with a renewed energy to be better and do more. The new nurse had worked hard to meet the needs but it seemed the clinic missed her presence. She was puzzled and when she prodded further, she discovered more than one client had told the clinic administrators that they preferred Katie because she always gave them a sense of hope and belief in themselves. They always felt respected and not judged. Upon hearing this Katie realized how important it was to be present and to listen with an open heart. Positive contributions toward emotional and mental well being were critically linked to physical health. However it wasn't until years later that Katie knew the key to effective nursing was simply the fundamental practice of caring, which was really just unconditional love wrapped in a particular type of package.

When Katie returned to her position, she continued to work hard to be productive and eventually caught more attention from the owners. They wanted to promote her to regional manager of three of their clinics so she could share her best practices with others. She was excited about the prospect of being able to put a down payment on a small house but she knew from past experience, she was not good at office politics. She was forever biting her tongue to keep the peace. Her head told her she would be crazy to reject the offer, while her heart was giving her grief about the decision. Old friends told her she was a bleeding heart and that she needed to get a better paying job, so she could purchase a nice home. Others wanted to know why such a smart woman like her, had settled and not gone on to become a doctor. Katie was feeling conflicted, especially about leaving behind people who needed her.

At the same time, a number of women who frequented her clinic had organized a rally to bring attention to the issues creating poverty. Most of those struggling were powerless and voiceless by themselves. Few had little energy to challenge the system while raising a family alone. It was risky to speak out and admit they were poor. Protesting could cause further harm by embarrassing their children and possibly alienating people who had been providing good will support. They were desperate and Katie knew she had to stand with them. She could no longer keep quiet but as a result of the picketing, she landed herself in the media. Now her old friends wanted to know why she was carelessly making a bad name for herself by causing trouble. Then her supervisor met with her to say that the committee had a change of heart. They decided she would not be a good ambassador for their clinics. The offer of a promotion had been withdrawn.

Katie's friends thought she had failed to launch, what could have been, a successful career. However she was secretly relieved. She finally felt at peace about speaking out against situations she felt were wrong. However no matter how much she feared the reprisals of the established powers or her social circles of conformity, it was imperative for her own sense of balance to wake up each morning with a clear conscience. Her new life was ripe with opportunity and choice between easy or hard, right or wrong, going along or standing alone. Layered in between were the expectations to conform to the status quo. It was hard for her to fit into the business of the rat race. She felt alienated from societal norms she saw as broken. Life was a constant challenge and she had learned a painful lesson, that you could not "rock the boat" if you wanted to get ahead.

She needed some time to centre herself and process what had happened. She returned home again to spend some time with her father. She longed for the solitude of her little island to rejuvenate her soul. Her connection to the land was like a reboot. Katie's world had grown bigger and every time she went home, the island seemed to get smaller. Sam always welcomed her with open arms and a face beaming with delight. Her bedroom had never changed and it was a return to a little bubble of separation from the real world. The gentle breezes that had cocooned and inspired her as a child, did not allow her to understand back then, what she now knew. Without innocence as a filter, she could see how the raging winds had tried to warn her about the lands far away. She confessed to Sam that she had failed. However he smiled and supported her as always. He told her that she was just being a good

Light Keeper.

Her father always had a way of making her feel better and simplifying the most complex dramas. This was another one of the reasons the town's folk valued her father's wisdom. Upon reflection she realized that she may have not met other people's definition of success but she did stay true to the people who needed her and her own sense of what was right. Perhaps the love that guides human hearts is the light that needs tending. Katie imagined herself, not as the person tending the beam of a lighthouse to warn seafarers, but as an ordinary person who carried an internal lantern, made brighter by well trimmed introspection and the oil of eternal love. Her lantern travelled with her into every life experience and if wielded with courage, could disperse evil hiding in the shadows.

Over supper one evening, Katie told her father the theory of the lantern bearer. She said that she did not really believe she was a superhero light slayer. The real impact would be in the ripples created by small acts of caring.

Sam replied, *"Ah, I see you have discovered your special powers and the family secret. Being a Light Keeper was never about the lighthouse. Your grandfather came to this island, as a place to hide. He craved solitude and believed it would save him from the madness of the world. He was eventually discovered by the town's folk and the lighthouse just happened to need a caretaker at that time."*

He added, *"I have always been proud of you Katie, there are a lot of us Light Keepers out there. You are never alone. Stay true to yourself. Stay the course. Remember to keep your light bright, however you can. The world needs us now more than ever".*

8 OH CANADA

Canada was Trent's "home and native land", "glorious and free". Trent and his wife were Canadians with two children and a lovely brick bungalow at the top of the small mountain overlooking a bay in a rural community. The nearby town was quaint but growing quickly and had spread out towards the highway with new construction and a busy retail commercial area. The museum where Trent worked was located downtown in one of the older historic buildings. Trent was responsible for obtaining the financial backing, not just for the staff and the exhibits, but also for the building itself. The province did help with grants, but the bulk of the money came from the town, the local historical committee, fundraising efforts and the entrance fees. The town and its museum relied on tourism dollars. However the pandemic, the high gas prices and unreliable transportation due to pandemic restrictions, had suppressed travel to the historic village.

Trent was not worried, this was Canada and everything would turn out fine. He sang the anthem with pride at special gatherings. He grew up with the flag like a child's comfort blanket with maple leaf on it. The government had promised emergency support funding. So today as on most days, Trent set off for work at the gallery and historic repository he had curated for the past decade. He always felt fortunate to have landed this position after completing his master's degree in history. It was a small archive with a showroom on the ground floor focused on the town's gold mining and seafaring history. He was lucky to be friends with the mayor at that time, who gave him the position despite the protest of a few influential town's folk who wanted it for themselves. He loved what he did despite the recent events that made it harder to find staff. Trent found himself working longer hours as a result.

Trent was not worried about the shortage of labour or the mounting pressure from the new mayor and the historical committee. In particular, he was being targeted by those committee members who continued to remain envious of his position. While his friend was mayor, those trouble makers did not get any air time and caused no problems for him. It seemed that the new mayor did not have Trent's back. Then with reductions in funding, Trent was squeezed between recycling old acquisitions or pushing out the plans for building maintenance. It was the deterioration of the building that had landed him in hot water this time. With the building so close to the ocean port, the paint had faded, the soffits were peeling and the signage was in disrepair. After one heated meeting, the son of one of Trent's naysayers was installed to look after the museum books, bypassing Trent's hiring authority.

Trent was a busy man, especially with the curve balls thrown his way in recent years. He had to work harder to find money for the aging institution that was so important to the town. However something else was happening. Beyond the recent changes in mood from the mayor's office and the newly installed employee, even his original supporters were cool towards him. In fact he felt some of his neighbours were avoiding him. His wife also noticed it and wondered if the pandemic was getting people down. Grocery prices had skyrocketed and although the government had provided emergency funding, many had fallen through the cracks. The economy had slowed but Trent was not worried. He had always managed to land on his feet no matter what life threw at him. For Trent, this was Canada, the land of opportunity, fairness for all and where neighbours helped one another.

Trent was a proud flag waver but he was also fully aware that Canada was not perfect. Historically the country has done terrible things against the indigenous people and continued to treat these and other racialized people unfairly. However he felt there were inquiries and commissions to shine a light on and try to right these injustices. Trent followed the media stories about issues around social justice from time to time, but for him, there were no alarm bells ringing, just passing stories of people who Trent could not relate to. They were "the marginalized, the racialized, the poor, the criminals, the junkies...the them". The lack of hard-core investigative journalism, left the stories empty, without faces, lacking any connection to Trent's reality. In the bigger picture of society, every Canadian knows they live in the best country in the world. Don't they?

Trent did not have the best relationship with the new accountant. He had trouble getting clear answers from him when asked for financial status and reporting. Trent had to know where the money was going and exactly what the bottom line looked like so he could plan accordingly. When he examined the books himself, the employee was offended. Trent saw some discrepancies he could not explain and when he asked details, he got the brush-off. Trent could not go to the mayor or committee, so as a last resort, he asked the police to look into it. Trent hoped that the young man was not doing anything wrong. However, ultimately, Trent was responsible and accountable for the entirety of the museum, its funding and all expenditures. The town mayor and committee had put him in a difficult position by going over his head to hire this accountant. Trent needed to get to the bottom of it.

Trent was not worried, but should have been. The officers he asked to look into the issue were not helpful. They admitted that they had found evidence of fraud but would not provide any details. Then a week later, he was shocked when the RCMP showed up with a search warrant for his office and a warrant for his arrest. Trent was dumbfounded and still in the dark about what was going on when he was sent home with a court ordered undertaking, to not return to his place of work. The town immediately terminated his contract and he was replaced by one of the people who had wanted his job all these years. He was eventually given a package of disclosure. It was in reviewing this material, with witness statements, that he saw who was behind the betrayal. For five years, naysayers had been "swatting" him, with false complaints to police, creating damaging files, without his knowledge or ability to respond.

Trent's call to the police for help, triggered his own arrest. The accountant claimed the fraud was done with Trent's authorization. Again Trent was not worried but should have been. Canada has one of the most fair justice systems in the world. He believed that if he just told the truth, it would get it sorted out. There was no evidence Trent took any money for personal use. His financial records would confirm that. Everyone knew this new staff member had a gambling problem and he believed it would not be hard to trace the money to the accountant. Furthermore the statements made by the witnesses were entirely hearsay, innuendo and gossip. That gossip had spread to his neighbours long before he knew anything, explaining their stand-offish behaviour. Despite the false rumours, Trent maintained an impeccable reputation. He could not be convicted by malicious gossip alone, could he?

Trent explained his entire story to the RCMP and told them how they had made a mistake. However, his explanations did not seem to make any impact. Trent eventually realized it was not that they did not believe him, they just did not care and were not interested in the facts. Trent's closest friends were outraged by this turn of events. However many people secretly felt, the police would not have charged him unless he had done something wrong, as most flag waving Canadians would. Once charged, it was as if he was already convicted and nobody believed anything he said. The police and prosecution had already decided he was guilty. The naysayers spent years laying that groundwork. The police and courts were only interested in getting their conviction and used their unlimited funding to do that using whatever underhanded means possible. He was floored to watch them willfully withhold disclosure and then influence and use unreliable witnesses that benefited by cooperating with police. They didn't care if they got the right man. Just any easy target would do. There was a complaint, they put someone away for it and the problem was solved.

Trent had initially obtained the advice of a lawyer, but the mounting legal fees would cost him his home. He tried negotiating on his own for a warning, a fine or a suspended sentence. The prosecution would only accept a guilty plea and Trent couldn't do that. Trent had no witnesses to call because the only witness was the accountant who was now testifying against him. During the trial, the complainants for the crown perjured themselves with emotionally charged statements of what they heard and believed. They made him out to be a monster. Trent could only dispassionately state that what they said was not true and he did not commit fraud. He tried to submit his financial statements in defence, but the evidence was rejected by the judge. He objected to the hearsay and showed discrepancies in witness testimonies. He demonstrated how each witness had something to gain from his conviction and that they were after his job.

For the first time, Trent was worried. He tried to show that this was a politically motivated conspiracy, but that theme was rejected by the judge. Trent believed the trial was unfair, even fixed. That belief was confirmed in his mind when he was found guilty of all charges. Then, despite letters of support from members of his community attesting to his good character and the fact that he had never been in trouble with the law before, he was sentenced to six months in jail. The sentencing brief read by the judge contained hearsay misinformation spewed from witness testimony as if it were the truth. This statement was regurgitated by the press and made public without taking into account his side of the story. Many of Trent's friends, family and supporters were disgusted. Others were confused and many of these and others, lost faith in the institutions they thought were fair and balanced.

While incarcerated, Trent discovered that more than half of the people in jail are still presumed innocent and waiting for a trial. Many plead guilty, just to end the wait and do the time as soon as possible, just to keep homes, jobs and relationships. Police and those in their circle, can destroy anyone they choose to, just by charging them and forcing them into "the system". Trent came to believe that Canada's justice system is perverted. Everything it does, is for the benefit of itself and those connected with it. Police feed jails with easy targets. Those convicted spend their life savings on lawyers. As incarcerations increase, government funding is expanded and funnelled for jobs and resources to areas such as Legal Aid, Corrections, Courts and Policing. Private savings and tax dollars together, creates a boom in business, justification for higher salaries and promotions for all those connected to the system, from arrest to parole.

Trent could no longer trust the justice system. This was not the Canada he had come to believe in. Not long ago, he looked down on police states and the failures in democracy to the south. Now he wondered, "are we any different?" A country's measure of greatness lies in the way it treats its vulnerable people. Yes, Canada is a safe haven for those from places of war, famine and persecution. Yes, Canada is generally a safe place, where most of us can get healthcare, education and live in peace. Yes, we are free to seek the career of our choice, but if we are not the right kind, we may not be hired. Yes, we can find a great job, but if the employer does not pay a living wage, we may need several jobs. While higher education is not affordable, healthcare is. However it is not accessible when wait times leave people dying in emergency waiting rooms. Trent no longer trusted the government's commitment to our best interests.

Trent could now see that, unless "glorious and free" is for everyone, none of us is truly free to live, with a clear conscience. We may be expected to hold "true patriot love" and believe with "glowing hearts" in a "true north-strong". Sadly however we are not "free" or do we remain "glorious". It is true "from far and wide" many with power and authority "stand on guard" but not always for what is best for others or for Canada. Canada Day has always been a day to celebrate without question. Trent could no longer be a hypocrite. After Trent's shock, denial, anger and failure at bargaining in truth, he could not trust his government, the police and was wary of those who say they are friends. Canadians are not always nice. On July 1st, instead of community events or fireworks, Trent now stays home. His flag permanently flies at half mast. As for the anthem, the best he can do is sigh, "Oh, Canada".

It was a long time before Trent found reasons to be hopeful. He managed to save his house, his marriage and get another job. It wasn't easy with a criminal record. While many friends stuck by him, his circle of friends had changed. Trent became increasingly encouraged by the way others, having been wise to the societal issues in Canada, have been stepping up, speaking out and making a difference. Half the battle of creating a better world is knowing that it is broken in the first place. The beliefs he had previously, were based on blind faith. His re-education was sad but necessary. Going forward Trent would do his homework and support those affected by injustices, in any way he could. Trent's Canadian fairy tale had ended. However it was replaced by something healthier, a healed woundedness fuelling a large dose of skepticism mixed with compassion and purpose.

Over time Trent learned to become increasingly hopeful, that with like minded others, they would "see thee rise, the True North strong and free". He accepted the idea that Canada was always and is always in the process of becoming. It had not arrived and never fully would for everyone. Canada is sparsely populated, over a large land mass of isolated communities, filled with fallible humans. All who have a penchant for narrow mindedness, self-centredness, greed and desire for power. It is what makes us human. The positive side is the deep well of optimism and the better aspects of our nature like kindness, empathy, generosity and a desire for fairness. What is "glorious" about Canada is our freedom to be hopeful and opportunities to express that better side of being Canadian. It is this core optimism in Trent that would eventually allow him to make peace and restore his pride in "O Canada".

9 HAL & OWEEN

Harold and his brother wanted to do something special on this particular night. They liked playing games in the house like hide and seek, but tonight was different. They could feel it in the air and they saw it happen every year over their most recent memories. It was a time for candy, tricks, scaring others and being frightened themselves. Harold wanted to dress up like some sort of monster that was green and slimy but was not sure how to achieve that. His little brother had all sorts of disgusting ideas that were either really messy or would smell bad. Little brother, Oween, wanted to be a fairy with wings and a wand. That would be much simpler to create.

They did not want anyone to know what they were planning. It would not be any fun if nobody was surprised or scared. So while everyone was out of the house doing the yard work and decorating, they got to work. Oween found some cardboard that he cut out and coloured to make wings. They were not very big ones and they were brown and black. He used a marker to draw veins on the wings. They ended up looking more like the wings of a giant insect rather than a fairy, but he was pleased with the results. He then found an old flour bag in the attic. It was huge because it had once contained one hundred pounds of flour. They don't make bags that size anymore. He cut out holes for his head and his arms and went to work colouring it with markers.

Meanwhile Harold was still trying to formulate a vision for what his monster would look like. He definitely wanted to be green. He managed to find an old sheet in the back of the linen closet that looked like it had not been used in a long time. He then went to the cupboard where he knew he would find lots of arts and craft supplies. There was a set of large, thirteen ounce, containers of Tempera paints that had been used for finger painting one time. He found two different greens, a lime and a forest green. That would do the trick. He laid the sheet out on the floor, dumped the paints on the cloth and started rubbing his hands around in it. His plan was to cover the cloth and make it all greenish but he made a terrible mess in the craft room.

Harold also decided he needed to have a big nose and some horns on his head. He found a pair of glasses with a fake nose and removed the nose part.

He then found some string to tie the nose on his face. That too got a coating of green paint. He went up into the attic to check on Oween. He was still colouring his flour sack in a rainbow of colours, to hide the writing. He was so intense in his concentration, he did not even look up when Harold arrived, looking for an old hat. He found one with a string that goes under the chin. He then borrowed some of Oween's leftover cardboard and took it downstairs. There he removed the brim and rolled the cardboard to make horns. He then glued those on to what was left of the hat and left it to dry.

They did not have a lot of time. It was nearing dark and soon it would be suppertime. It got dark so quickly this time of year. The paint was not dry yet but Harold could not wait. He splashed green paint on the hat and horns, cut one hole in the sheet for his head and two holes for his arms. He then tied the nose and hat on his face and head. He headed upstairs to get Oween who was just finishing off his own costume by using clothespins to hold the wings on. He didn't hear Harold coming and let out a blood curdling scream when he turned around and saw the green monster. Harold had made such a mess that even his face, pants and shoes were coated in various colours of green blotches. Harold was so surprised by Oween's reaction, he screamed too. Then they both took to a fit of laughter. He told Oween to hurry up.

Harold went back down and grabbed the kit of

Tempera paints and carried them up to the attic. He dabbed some on Oweens face as per his instructions. Some, red, blue and yellow dabs on his forehead, chin and nose. Harold helped his little brother into the flour bag and made sure his wings were secured. As they started down the stairs, they heard a commotion in the kitchen. The others had returned and were talking in hushed tones. Oween stopped mid step and told Harold that he forgot his wand. They both went back up into the attic and rummaged around for something to use. Oween found an old hockey stick that had the end broken off. He quickly used some of the Tempera paints to dab the hockey stick as well. Oween thanked his big brother "Hal" for helping him. When Harold was younger he was called Hal but always hated that short form. Now that he was older, he insisted on being called Harold, however Oween could never remember.

Then, they tiptoed down the stairs. There were certain steps that creaked when stepped on. It was a game they used to play to avoid being heard when they were sneaking around the house. They knew this house well. The two of them knew every nook and cranny of this old farm house. There was a dirt basement where vegetables were stored for the winter in sawdust bins. There was a milk separating machine and a butter churner that they watched the being using a number of times. There was also a place in the basement to hang game like rabbit, before they were cleaned. The most imposing item was the wood furnace. Every morning somebody had to get up earlier than the rest and make a fire to heat the house before others got out of bed. The heat would rise up through grates in the floor to the second story and melt the ice on the inside of the old windows.

They love the cubby-hole that was curtained off under the ground floor stairwell. It was a great place to hide and play where nobody could see them. At the top of the stairs on the second floor were four large bedrooms. One bedroom was not totally finished so you could squeeze behind the wall and under the eves where there was more storage. Then, hidden in a closet, was a smaller set of stairs leading to the attic. That was the best place of all. They were not allowed up there but they would sneak up anyway when the others were busy. The attic had lots of old furniture and trunks filled with pictures, mementos and old clothes. Sneaking upstairs is where they learned how to navigate around the creaky steps without being found out. However in the excitement of this evening, they forgot themselves and the stairs betrayed them with three loud squeaks.

They rushed towards the first level, avoided the kitchen and bolted out the front door. They scrambled down the front steps and hid in the bushes. The others had decorated the place well when they were outside. There were three jack-o-lanterns on the stairs with candles flickering in the breeze. The bush they hid behind, next to the stairs, was covered in webbing and spiders. The door knocker had been transformed to a skeletal hand. The front lawn had a collection of artificial graves with hands and skulls coming out of the ground, while fake ghosts floated from tree branches. The sun had just set and as the street lights came on, the yard took on an eerie green glow. At least that is what Harold thought as he looked through the layers of green paint splattered all over his face. Oween and Harold tried to hide quietly outside but could not help themselves. They started to giggle every time they looked at one another. They wanted to be the first to arrive at the door so they could get their prank in early. They had other places to go tonight if they wanted candy.

They could hear the others in the house going room to room and talking excitedly. They seemed upset about something. There was a mess of paints in the craft room as if the paint containers had exploded somehow. A trail of paint drips went all the way to the attic stairs. One person swore to the others that she heard someone up in the attic rummaging around after hearing a loud scream and laughter. Someone else admitted that they heard it too. It even sounded like someone was creeping down the stairs when the steps squeaked. They had to extinguish the jitters and calm down so they could finish preparing supper. There was still much to do. They had to finish some of the indoor decorating, clean up the paint mess and put out the candy. It was important to have everything ready because once they started coming, there was not much time for anything else. Then as supper was placed on the table they rounded everyone up.

When those inside had settled down to eat, Harold and Oween creeped up to the front door and rang the doorbell. When the door opened, there was another bloodcurdling scream. The person who opened the front door was caught off guard. They were sure they saw a life sized insect and a green goblin on the front steps. The boys were ecstatic, that was exactly the reaction they were hoping for. It was mayhem as everyone inside came rushing to the door. The boys used the confusion to quickly brush past them and hide inside again. What everybody saw was just a pile of coloured fabric, an old hat and a hockey stick. It was obviously a prank. They had all been rattled. Everyone was jumpy on this hallowed eve and more so after this evening's events.

They laughed it off and as they were finishing up their dessert, again they heard something. The mother and father and their two teenage girls had moved into the house last year and were still trying to get familiar with the odd sounds an old house can make. One turned to the others and asked *"can you hear that?"* The others gulped and nodded in agreement. Even their dog Muffin had pricked up her ears and was tilting her head side to side, listening intently. There it was. It could not be mistaken. The muffled sounds were of children's laughter and giggles, specifically reminiscent of two young boys.

They searched all the rooms including the attic where they found more evidence of paint and a disturbance. They combed every room and every nook and cranny and could not find any children hiding anywhere. The sounds could still be heard and when the awful conclusion was reached, everyone's skin turned into a raised bed of goosebumps. The voices were coming from inside the walls of their old farmhouse. It was Hal and Oween.

10 STARGAZER

Darcy was a tall, wispy haired, no-nonsense academic who was haunted by an irrational belief that she had a special purpose, a calling. She endorsed the idea of an afterlife and the everlasting quality of souls. She often found herself looking up at the stars, hoping to see signs or miracles. She was on a mission to get to the bottom of this strange longing. She even visited a medium for insights from the other side. But nothing otherworldly ever happened. No apparitions, visions, dramatic awakening or visits from above. Darcy had just received her Bachelor of Arts degree and could take a management job near home, or do something completely different. She had spent much of her life studying and now she had arrived. But the anti-climax was unbearable. She wasn't ready to settle down and had nobody special in her life. She needed to find herself, whatever that meant, and understand her destiny.

Darcy always wanted to travel to Spain and rented an apartment in Sitges, on the Mediterranean coast southwest of Barcelona. She enrolled in a month-long Spanish language class at a small private school, just a ten minute walk into town. After three hours of in-class study every morning, followed by a siesta, she had the rest of the day to explore. She found an ocean-side cabana situated on a cliff overlooking a private beach with a stone patio and bistro style tables and chairs. In May the weather was warm enough for her to sit outside and enjoy the catch of the day with sangria. She relished the scenic views of the blue-green sea and the antique town with white stucco, clay roofs, blue accents, fuchsia vines and a winding seawall that terminated, in the far distance, at an ancient Baroque church. It was a peaceful spot in the off season and she longed for some solitude and reflection.

However that hope was short-lived. Within days of her arrival Darcy became involved with classmates Lorna from Ireland and Matthias from Belgium. Both had arrived in Sitges at the same time as she. Lorna had green eyes and was a fire-ball of energy. Matthias was always game for a new adventure and was on a break from law school and his fiance. Upon the urging of these two, Darcy could not resist the lure of excitement and fun. For the next four weeks they spent late nights and the wee hours of mornings, exploring clubs looking for the best blue cocktails, tapas and dance venues open until six am. Just before the last week of classes, Darcy told Lorna she needed a break. She had planned to do some writing and learn how to meditate. Lorna told her that she was actually preparing a pilgrimage over the original Camino Primitivo trail through the mountains in the north.

Lorna had already sourced out camping gear, hiking boots and had booked the hostels. She was able to book an additional spot and implored Darcy to join her. The two week trip promised beautiful scenic mountains, placid country sides, good food and a chance to explore many unique historical villages. The destination was Santiago de Compostela where James, the patron saint of Spain was buried. Darcy's interest was piqued. So after the three of them finished their classes in Sitges, they said goodbye to Matthias with lots of hugs and promises to keep in touch. Together they set out by train and soon were strolling along Las Ramblas of Barcelona, brimming with shops, restaurants, open air patios and street performers. Then they travelled on to Oviedo, where the real work of the trip began as they immediately changed focus from site-seeing to footwear, drinking water, their packs and finding a rhythm and a pace that allowed regular intervals of rest that worked for them.

There were wonderful places along the way to

taste regional and local foods, fresh cheeses, cava and be greeted by helpful people along the way. There was little talking while walking but the group always came together for a big meal, at the designated stopovers. Even though the trail was the same, no two people recalled the similar events or experienced their day in the same way. Darcy made a point of visiting the Basilicas and chapels to see the frescoes, paintings, sculptures, stained glass and artwork venerating Saints, Christ and the Virgin Mary. She especially sought out the sites of miracles. Lorna grew up with stories of fairies, surrounded by magic and was more interested in the people she met, their way of life and the natural surroundings. Lorna was delighted with her progress and felt rejuvenated. Darcy however was preoccupied with how her prayers had always seemed to evaporate into a void. Her disappointment in uncovering proof of the unseen, left her feeling conflicted and irritable.

By day five, when asked how she was doing, Darcy could only comment how her boots were too tight or how she had an upset stomach because of something she ate. She had become obsessed with the time and how long, before the next rest spot. There was nothing to do but walk and think. She continued to reflect on her past accomplishments but did not know how to transition that into a plan for the future. She did not know who she was, what she wanted or where she was going. Wandering aimlessly on this trail was not helping. Her mind was driving her crazy and her feet were hurting. The monotony was taking its toll on her mental stability and she felt it was a mistake to come on this pilgrimage. On day six, after a steep climb of over 1000 feet, to O Acevo, she could no longer hide her despair. She burst into tears and refused to walk any further.

Darcy told Lorna she needed to be alone, not to wait and to continue on without her. Lorna was reluctant to do so but Darcy insisted she would be fine and would catch up with her in a few days. After an emotional parting, Darcy found a quiet place at the edge of the road, overlooking a valley in the Cantabrian Mountains. No matter how she tried to quiet herself, thoughts were running rampant and triggering a cavalcade of emotions. She was feeling hopeless, angry, jealous of the others who seemed to be at peace with themselves and depressed, all at the same time. It was late afternoon and she took a path that led to a picnic table nestled in a small patch of trees overlooking a quiet rolling pasture. She found the sheltered spot calming. However by the time she was ready to go back to the only public cafe in the area, it was getting dark and she could no longer see the path.

When she realized her predicament, she became alarmed. She decided to just go back to the table and hope someone would come looking for her. However when she realized she did not tell anyone where she was going, Darcy began to feel desperate and afraid. She wrapped herself in a blanket from her pack and prayed, hoping this time, there was a God that would hear her. She looked up at the stars but did not get a chance to finish her petition, when she heard a bell tinkling. A sheep appeared on the path coming down the hill towards her, followed by a small herd, two Border Collies, and a man carrying a gas lantern and holding the hand of a little girl. They were surprised to see her there. She told them her story and they insisted that she stay with them for the night. It was going to be very cold at this high altitude and the cafe had closed for the evening.

The child appeared to be about seven years old. She announced excitedly, in broken English, that she had an extra bed in her room where the lady could stay. Together they made their way further down into the valley and just as dark descended completely, Darcy could see a small cottage ahead with lights in the windows, next to a paddock and small barn. The little girl took her by the hand into the kitchen and told her mother what happened, while the father closed up the barn for the night. The family was accustomed to meeting pilgrims passing through this area. The Camino Way was no easy feat. It was physically and emotionally demanding. Not everyone could make it to the planned stopovers and the locals felt it was their duty to keep the pilgrims safe. They were always prepared to welcome any strangers that might need their assistance.

After she had butifarra sausage and warm lamb stew with the family, they retired to the living area next to the fireplace. Darcy was yawning so the mother made up the guest room and showed her where everything was. She did not have to share a room with the little girl after all, who had already said goodnight an hour before. Just as Darcy was getting settled in, she heard a small knock at the door. It was the little girl who sneaked out of her room to present her with her special stuffed friend, so she wouldn't feel lonely in the night. It was a Raggedy Ann just like the red haired doll Darcy had growing up. Just like her, the little girl seemed to be an only child. She wondered if this little girl was praying for a sister like she had at that age. Relieved, she contemplated her luck as she rested her tired body and sore feet in a place that was comfortable and safe.

As she lay awake, recalling the emotional turmoil and replaying the detailed events of the day, a gigantic wave of gratitude washed over her. She could be freezing alone in the dark but she was rescued instead. Was this an answer to her prayer? The Raggedy Ann doll took her back to her lonely childhood and her unanswered prayers for a sister. Then she thought about Lorna who had been like a sister to her since they met in Sitges. Lorna even looked like the doll with her dark red hair and Bohemian style clothing. Despite the memories of solitude, the doll was oddly comforting and familiar. Then as she moved her focus to the emotional stirring within her, she heard a voice. It was not the same one that filled her brain with chatter. This soft utterance assured her she was never alone. She fell asleep feeling deeply loved in that moment, surrounded by a sense of warmth and she imagined a caring spirit had enveloped her in safety.

Over the next three days Darcy's mental well being and physical energy greatly improved as she continued the trail alone. On day seven, her hiking boots malfunctioned as the sole separated from the boot. A couple walking past her, saw what had happened, took her to a local cobbler and invited her to their home for lunch until she was reacquainted with her hiking footwear. On day eight she missed the yellow arrow and shell marker. She had been happily daydreaming and wandered off the trail. She spent a delightful time watching a soccer match instead. Some of the fans that were her own age, wanted a chance to practice their English and gave her a tour of the area before dropping her back at her scheduled rest stop for the evening. By day nine, Darcy had found that she could calm her crazy mind chatter by focusing on her heart-self, counting her blessings and finding some reason to be grateful.

Lorna learned that she was getting closer to her group, from reports of the locals and the encouraging notes left for her by Lorna at the auberges. She noticed that the more thankful she felt, the more she could see how much she had been blessed. By the tenth evening, she was able to catch up with Lorna and the rest of the group. That evening the entire group met at a small restaurant near the old Roman wall of the city of Lugo. Everyone was tired but happy to sit down to a ten course feast of cold and hot soups, stews, boiled potato, octopus, beans, churros and beer. Lorna was relieved to see her and gave her a big hug as she walked through the door of the restaurant. Lorna was pleased to see she was physically intact but was concerned about her emotional state. Darcy assured her she was significantly better. Lorna could see from Darcy's calm demeanor and frequent smiling that something had changed.

Over the next couple of days, Darcy and Lorna had fun imagining all sorts of miracles, like the way someone would come by and offer fresh water just as they needed it, or how they had a craving for a particular pizza that would appear on the menu at the next stop. This spirited fun made the last two days of the trek memorable, as they joyously arrived at the tomb of Saint James. Very late that same evening, they found an outdoor bistro in Santiago with a view of the ostentatious twin spires of the Romanesque Basilica, to stop for a celebratory drink and make plans for what they would do next. As they both looked up at the same time they saw golden orbs of light moving erratically above the church. Speechless, they stared at each other as two excited male pilgrims, who had also finished the trail earlier that day, rushed over to their table to see if they saw the same phenomena.

A lively discussion ensued as the four continued to talk until morning, not wanting the enjoyable night to end. Darcy was attracted to the blond from England and the dark haired Irishman was interested in Lorna. Darcy was reminded of the story of Saint James whose tomb had been lost until a hermit saw lights dancing over the lost grave site. Darcy had been gazing at the stars all her life and now she too had seen strange lights. However, it was not the miraculous that changed her life. It was the gift of grace that opened her heart to new vistas on that stressful day six of her walk. She was no longer a confused, lonely, lost academic whose life was driven by goals and expectations of others to be someone. Now she just wanted to enjoy the present moment. Only time would tell what other surprises were in store for her and she viewed the future with excitement as she anticipated what might happen next. Darcy had found herself after all and that had changed everything.

11 THE TEACHER

Carolyn was in her last year of a mathematics program but was missing a couple of credits. She wanted to take something completely different so she managed to get into a more advanced class of social psychology. This course was about the mind, relationships, personalities, social influences and group behaviours. After so much advanced algebra, calculus and theoretical methodologies, she wanted a break from cold, impassioned numbers. This was definitely something that was less black and white and she wanted to challenge herself in a different way. It had been years since she had focused on the arts, this would be a piece of cake or so she thought. However she had no idea of the world of learning she was about to encounter, not just in the classroom.

As humans we tend to gravitate towards people who are just like us. Her math friends had been with her for the past three years and were dependable and predictable. They all liked the same movies, games and had become a tight group with similar opinions and outlooks on life. When Carolyn stepped into the psychology class, she was immediately struck by the diversity of students in the class. Because most were in the arts and humanities, not only was the course material new, so was the mix of personalities. That is something she had not considered when signing up. There were students of all ages, some were dressed in suits while others wore dreadlocks and sported bare feet in class. Like her group of math nerds, as others called them, they too had formed cliques and groups of friendships. She found it interesting to watch the various interactions.

As much as she tried to keep to herself, the professor was big on group projects. Carolyn was an outsider but was quickly adopted by a group of five rambunctious, argumentative friends who were close to her age. They knew each other well and were very interested in learning more about her, much to her discomfort. The five included Karen, Beth, Ingrid, Deitmar and Kayichi. Karen was the quiet one that was extremely polite and always smiling. Beth was tall with a mop of curly hair who was loud and enjoyed telling everyone else what to do. Ingrid was from Iceland and staying in the International House on campus. Dietmar was a vegan with strong opinions about eating meat while Kayichi was from Japan, where his parents operated a dairy farm. They were all psychology majors and were avid readers, always competing about who read the latest published articles or what teachers and teachings they aligned with and why.

It had been a couple of months and Carolyn had become comfortable in her group. Dietmar was planning to go into the priesthood and was always being challenged by his friends about religion. He wanted all of the group to accompany him on a three day pilgrimage to a Benedictine monastery near Magog Quebec. Because everyone had given him such a hard time about the priesthood, he said they owed him big time. It was going to be a hiking extravaganza and he said that he expected all his friends to support him in this. Plus a well known catholic priest who was a famous psychology author and researcher in the area of spirituality, community and social justice, would be a guest speaker at the Abbey, hosted by L'Arche. According to all five of her classmates, this guy was a big deal. That opportunity to learn from one of their "greats", was enough to convince all of them, including Carolyn, to sign up for this pilgrimage.

The thought of meeting this famous researcher was not enticing but intimidating for Carolyn. What interested her the most were the pictures of the Appalachian mountains and the beautiful hardwood trees. The trip would be physically challenging as they had to walk all day, uphill and then stay overnight at the Abbey. That sounded exhilarating and she knew she would enjoy seeing the vistas and getting the fresh air. Touring a monastery was also a bonus since they rarely allowed visitors. There were many people from the university who were also going and the bus was full on that Saturday morning of the Thanksgiving weekend. The air was buzzing with conversation and laughter. The closer they got to their destination, the more rural it became and the trees were showing their colours more brilliantly than they did near Toronto. The final stop was actually at the base of a ski resort and it was these trails they would follow up the mountain. The guides for the trip were members of a catholic group from campus who had organized this outing.

There were people of every age here and as the group collected their gear, some of the guides came around to make sure everyone had water and the proper footwear. Before they began, the guides reminded them this was a religious pilgrimage for many attendees and that they should refrain from talking while walking, to respect other people's need for silence. They could however, on the scheduled rest stops, engage in conversation at that time. So that is what most of the hikers did. Karen and Kayichi and Carolyn had no trouble with being quiet but Beth, Ingrid and Dietmar were constantly breaking out into chatting and whispering until Dietmar hushed them up. Carolyn could hear the odd argument and she would look over at Karen who was biting her lip to keep from laughing. Carolyn and Kayichi however were just annoyed with their friends.

From a distance Carolyn suspected they looked like an army of dark coloured ants winding its way up the side of a light coloured granite mountain dotted with yellow birch and speckled with red and orange maples. When they stopped part way up there was a resting place with a small lodge and picnic tables. Most congregated with the groups they had been travelling with and sat in circles on the ground. There were parents with children, other students and a few older folk. The view from this location was spectacular with nothing but the rolling hills, mountains and trees enveloping an expansive lake. Carolyn found the hardest part was climbing over and around all the granite boulders. Her feet however were OK and her choice of hiking boot was appropriate. She just wanted to rest her feet in peace and have something to drink. That expectation was not going to be fulfilled.

Carolyn's psychology friends had become fully engaged in an argument that had begun between Ingrid and Beth on the way up the mountain. One believed we were born with a free will and the other said there was no such thing because of our genetic and cultural programming. One said that because of free will man can shape his own destiny, while the other protested that our choices are limited. Dietmar had also been a part of the earlier discussion between shushing them. He piped in that acknowledging the existence of one's soul was the determining factor in free will. An older gentleman who Carolyn had noticed sitting alone on the bus, gravitated towards her group and the psychological discussion. Her group was friendly, welcomed him and told him that they were in their final year of their respective degrees. The gentleman asked Carolyn about her thoughts on the topic but Beth told him that Carolyn was no psychology major.

Beth suggested that the gentleman ask Dietmar what he thought since he was a psychology major and was also going into the priesthood. The man seemed impressed and then turned to everyone and asked what they thought about how much man is guided by his own nature versus the environment in which he is nurtured. That question just further ramped up the animation of the group. Beth gave her opinion without giving others a chance to speak. Ingrid got louder as she tried to speak over Beth's voice. Dietmar tried to referee the two dominant debaters and facilitate Beth's attempts to speak, while Kayichi just listened. Carolyn was happy to have been deemed as not being qualified to have any relevant thoughts about psychology and stepped out of the discussion altogether. The older gentleman enjoyed the heated exchange and seemed almost pleased with what he started.

Carolyn was not sure what she thought

anyway and was more interested in watching the group dynamics at play in this real life example of what she had been learning in class. She also wondered who this man was, what his background was and why he was so interested in psychology. The gentleman was genuinely and intensely interested in her classmates' ideas. She also wondered why he was on this trip. Each person had their own personal reasons to partake in a pilgrimage. Nobody in her group asked the man who he was and what he thought even though he raised the question. The group saw themselves as the experts in the area of psychology. So her group just ran with the topic that was introduced and did what they always did in the same way they always behaved. Like Carolyn and Kayichi, the gentleman seemed happy to be excluded from the discussion and just listen.

Carolyn was learning a lot about group dynamics in this psychology elective. Her tight knit friends displayed their usual performance. Beth was the leader. Ingrid challenged that and thought she knew better than Beth. Dietmar was the mediator who was happy to follow a leader as long as he made them work for it. Karen was the outlier who did not always agree with the others. Often when she tried to carefully frame her opposing ideas, she would be shot down, clam up and bite her lip. Karen reluctantly agreed to disagree, in favour of preserving her relationships within the group. Carolyn sensed that Kayichi was afraid of the others and his need for acceptance was more important than his own voice. If anyone persisted in challenging Beth, she would use her grades and credentials as a co-author on a published research paper to bolster her dominance. Then if group consensus continued to be threatened, the argument sank to the level of personal insults that amounted to bullying.

The gentleman enjoyed the discussion and thanked the psychology students for their candid thoughts and valuable insights. As everyone got ready to take to the trail again, the gentleman nodded towards her and smiled as he moved on to speak with another group of young people. The guides came around and checked on everyone's progress and advised that the next leg of the journey would be slightly more challenging. They expected to reach the monastery in time for a late evening meal. Then they would each be billeted for the night at the hostels on location. The next morning would be the tour of the facilities and after lunch they would listen to the guest lecturer. The world renown dutch priest-psychologist, former Yale and Harvard award winning teacher, lecturer and prolific author, who was now working with vulnerable groups through the L'Arche organization, would be giving a talk about his life work. Her friends were excited about the prospect of hearing this man speak. After all their talk about this man, Carolyn was looking forward to this as well.

The final trek up the mountain was both steep

and rocky. It had to be taken slowly which gave plenty of opportunity to look across the mountain and down into the lake below. The landscape was unspoiled by man and was breathtaking to see. As they neared the apex, Carolyn could see the Abbey's steeples, a large bell tower and two smaller architectural towers. The pilgrims arrived at approximately 4 pm and that gave Carolyn a chance to explore the grounds and apple orchard. The Abbey was a large complex of buildings and looked like a modern day castle. The architecture inside was spectacular with high vaulted ceilings, arches, hallways, stained glass and art work. The supper was served on long tables by the monks. They had carrot soup, served with bread, cheese, chicken pot pie with roasted potatoes and apple crisp for dessert. Everything including the cheese and cider was made by the monks who followed a strict regime of prayer, participation in mass, work and study. Talking was limited and the place was silent except for the deep melodious and inspirational Gregorian chanting heard in the distance.

As soon as the meal was over, everyone was escorted to their respective hostels for the overnight stay. The nuns ran the women's hostel. Beth, Ingrid, Karen and Carolyn said goodbye to Dietmar and Kayichi as they made their way to their individual rooms, fitting for a monastery. Each room had a single bed, desk, chair and one large window. There was a light on the table and clean towels on the bed.

The washrooms and showers were shared. The accommodations were austere but clean, They were exhausted but despite that Carolyn got up early the next morning. She was excited and wanted to explore. Not all areas were open to the public. The church was open so she spent some time there until the others started gathering for breakfast. Carolyn thought she saw the gentleman they met on the trail, in the church earlier. She had wanted to at least ask him his name but she didn't see him at breakfast.

Dietmar was excited to hear the lecture and their group left the meal early to get front row seats in the auditorium. After everyone else filed in and sat down behind them, Carolyn spotted the gentleman near the side of the stage. He smiled with recognition as he nodded towards her group. As they recognized him, they were all somewhat confused to see him wearing a long cassock. Dietmar leaned over to Carolyn and grinned saying that the gentleman must be trying to get into the feel of the place by dressing the part. The excitement built up when the monsignor for the Abbey took to the microphone. They thought this was their great teacher, however he only welcomed them to the monastery and then introduced the teacher. As their gentleman friend took the stage, Beth, Ingrid, Dietmar, Beth and Kayichi all turned to each other, speechless, with their mouths wide open, as their jaws dropped to the floor.

The light bulb had finally flickered on as

Carolyn listened to this humble and articulate man speaking about his work with the vulnerable, inclusivity and compassion. She could not stop thinking about how she and the others had fallen into a group mentality. They had become so wise in their own eyes that they had become insulated and could not see beyond their own bubble. They had travelled all this way to meet someone who had been in their midst all along. Carolyn regretted not asking the questions that had been presenting themselves in her mind. Her acceptance of the opinions of others, who downplayed her knowledge, caused her to take a back seat to her own wisdom. She was not alone, she could see her friend's looks of bewilderment as they too examined their own regrets. As a math major, stepping out into a new field of study was eye opening. She never expected to learn and experience so much. This was the best elective, in all her university years, worth more than a couple of credits. The dumbfounded looks on her classmate's faces alone, was priceless.

12 WHISPERERS

OMG Jonathan, had done it again. He had only left the yard for ten minutes. Now he was in trouble with his mother again. Their neighbourhood was originally designed, so folks could easily visit one another and there were still some gates between the fenced yards. The entire subdivision was built on the old Wary farmland. Jonathan's property backed on to the rear of the original house, built before indoor plumbing. The white clad and brick, two storied structure, had two peaks, a large covered veranda on the front and an enclosed porch on the back. The corners where the roof and pillars met, were decorated with gingerbread style wooden carvings. The barn was long gone but an old red shingled garage, at the back of the property, still contained some antique farm equipment. The new subdivision consisted of two main streets of seventies style bungalows and a growing number of modern homes, with the farmhouse at one end and a park at the other.

Jonathan's yard still had a shared gate. He was making his way back toward the old waist high, grey picket fence and as he stepped through the gap, he saw her. Their eyes locked briefly as he tenuously glanced towards the rear kitchen window, at the same time his mother was gazing out over their overgrown backyard. He was supposed to be mowing, weeding and watering the garden. His father was away on business and his mother had a long list of to-do's she wanted completed, in the next three days. However, Jonathan couldn't bear to see Mrs. Wary struggling to get the top off her garbage bin. She had tied it down with a bungee cord to keep the raccoons out but it had gotten twisted and her hands were too weak to get it untangled. She often made homemade peanut butter cookies or his favourite blueberry apple pie. Today, after freeing the lid, it was chocolate chip cookies.

A big storm was coming, not just weather wise. Today Jonathan got caught eating cookies at Mrs. Wary's house before finishing his own chores. His mother was wild with him. Plus he was worried about an issue with Billy that had been brewing at school for a while. Jonathan did not trust Billy who was spending a lot of time with his friends, whispering and snickering in Jonathan's direction. Last week, Billy told everyone that Jonathan had stolen a calculator from the sixth grade classroom when Jonathan saw Billy take it himself. He knew what his father would tell him to do. He had been thinking long and hard about what action he would take. He just needed to muster the resolve to get on with it. Finally, on the last day of school, Jonathan ventured to the south side next to the gymnasium, where he spied Billy sneaking a cigarette with his newest buddies.

Jonathan stepped determinedly into the circle, squarely faced Billy and asked him what his problem was. Billy was six inches taller than Jonathan and was surprised by Jonathan's directness. Only momentarily unnerved, Billy smoothly regained his prowess, laughed and blew smoke in Jonathan's face, pretending he did not know what Jonathan was talking about. As a larger crowd gathered and seeing he had a bigger audience, Billy grabbed Jonathan's shoulder, called him a shrimp and asked him what he was going to do about it. Jonathan stepped closer without losing eye contact and questioned Billy about the lies. Jonathan believed Billy was a coward and was hoping he was right. He was and it worked. Billy walked away mumbling something about not wanting to hurt a pathetic little kid. Jonathan was relieved and felt he could put this concern to rest, for now.

With school over, Jonathan was looking forward to reconnecting with friends. The annual May pot-luck barbecue was a perfect event for a reboot. During the afternoon preparations, after successfully delivering his mother's potato salad contribution,

Jonathan climbed his favourite red maple and found a comfortable spot. Just as he was about to fall asleep, ten adults huddled around the picnic table at the base of his tree. They darted their eyes about to make sure they were out of ear shot before lowering their voices and whispering among themselves. Nobody looked up. Some sounded angry, there were urgent comments and hushing by others. The new neighbour, who had moved into the biggest house on their block, spoke insistently about his property value and the Wary situation. Jonathan could not make out much, but he did know, it was not good and it involved Mrs. Wary.

A week later a neighbour from across the street had come by to deliver some used clothes for his younger twin sisters. At one point, the conversation took a judgmental turn and his mother was disapprovingly questioned, as to why she allowed Jonathan to visit Mrs. Wary. His mother quickly changed the topic but he overheard her retelling the event over the phone to her best friend, saying how annoyed she was with how this neighbour was meddling in her business. Jonathan also heard the Wednesday night cribbage ladies say they were only reporting what they heard, out of concern for Mrs. Wary. Then in a low, baleful, gravelly voice, someone stated that her yard was unkempt and her house always dark. Even younger kids at school were in a frenzy about how Scary Wary's house was haunted. Something was not right, the whispering was wrong, the adults were keeping it a secret and Mrs. Wary was being bullied.

Jonathan noticed a number of neighbours had stopped being friendly to Mrs. Wary by no longer smiling or waving at her. Mrs. Wary was the nicest, most caring lady he knew. She was like a second mother to him. Up until this summer, he spent a lot of time helping her around the yard. When he was much younger, she read stories to him and encouraged him to read and to do well in school. She had five grandkids, some around his age, but they lived far away. She missed them and said she was happy to borrow Jonathan every so often. Her yard was a fun and cheerful place with a colourful display of antiques, bird feeders, whirligigs, wind-chimes, patches of berries and giant sunflowers. There was also a faded red and white flag on her front porch with dragons, crosses and a top hat. It was her family emblem with "Je Trouve Bien", translated as "I Find Good", written at the top.

On the Friday before the July 1st long weekend, Jonathan's mother sent him down to the local convenience store to pick up more milk. Jonathan had been thinking about Mrs. Wary and just as he walked in, he saw her at the checkout packing up a large purchase. She was pleased to see him and he arrived just in time to help her with the bags. As always, Mrs. Wary wanted to know how he was doing at school. He immediately said great and then paused and gave her an abridged version of the Billy issue.

She sighed and said she was sorry he had to experience that. She was proud of the thoughtful and brave way he approached the problem. Mrs. Wary said that being bullied happens to the best of us whether you are a young person in school, an experienced adult in the prime of your career or an old person, living a quiet life in an ordinary neighbourhood.

Nothing else was said between them about bullying. He suspected Mrs. Wary was aware of what was going on in the neighbourhood and Jonathan could not help thinking about it. He did more research and learned that the newest neighbour, Billy's father, wanted to improve the standards of everyone in the community. He had put a lot of money into property upgrades and had the largest and fanciest house in the area. However he would never see a return on his investment unless the entire neighbourhood improved. Most of the original families had moved away and the new ones had no attachment to the farm and the history of the subdivision. The Wary property with meadows, not lawns, outbuildings and an old style house, decorated with doodads of every colour, belied any allegiance to the present generation. The farmhouse no longer fit with the modern community surrounding it.

Mrs. Wary had lived there for over six decades. She did not have the energy or desire to upgrade, get rid of the front garden or her beloved treasures and memories. Everything was in working order and she had a small group of families who she could rely on, like Jonathan's. She and now a minority of neighbours, did not see the need to keep up with the expensive cars, bigger additions, open concept kitchens and en-suite master bedrooms. Their fourteen hundred square foot homes, with three bedrooms and one and a half bathrooms, were enough. They were happy with their smaller, easier to heat homes, mature trees, extensive gardens and flowering bushes of every colour. They did not mind seeing laundry drying on clotheslines, ongoing car repairs in driveways or wood being piled high along yards to provide an alternative heat source, for those lucky enough to have wood stoves.

The neighbourhood had developed into a mixture of styles and philosophies with the older properties being in the minority. Some could not believe Mrs. Wary still had an old outhouse on the property, while others felt her decorating style was an eyesore. A few fought to have many of the old trees, lining the street, removed because of the mess made by the falling leaves. Some complained about pollution every time wood smoke was detected coming from a chimney. Others loudly commented about how old shrubbery on several properties should be removed to make way for more tasteful landscaping. The new neighbour had successfully campaigned against Mrs. Wary's way of life in the name of progress. Many that joined the gentrification bandwagon, did not know Mrs. Wary as a person and did not care about putting down roots as much as eventually flipping a house for profit.

Jonathan thought long and hard about the neighbourhood issue. Mrs. Wary was his friend and in a situation like this, where the bullying is secretive and underhanded, a third party needed to take action. Jonathan started a list of points and rehearsed what he was going to say when the time was right. Later that week, he overheard his mother tell his father about a meeting to discuss urban renewal. He burst in on the conversation and insisted that they take him to that meeting, that he was not just a kid and he should have a say, like everyone else. Surprised, his mother told him to stop being ridiculous. His father however was intrigued and said that Jonathan's interest in this proves he has grown up. Jonathan's father wanted to know what his son had to say and felt he had a right to say it, whatever it was.

That Friday, Jonathan and his father drove to the local volunteer fire station while his mom stayed home with the girls. The whisperers from the May barbecue were seated at a table along the front of the hall. Many people were filing in to fill the forty, folding plastic chairs, set up in rows. There was a microphone on a stand, in the center aisle, for questions. The audience listened to anecdotal evidence of how other communities had protected their land and property investments, by adopting restrictive covenants and committees to approve changes to individual properties. Eventually someone asked about a certain old property and what could be done. When the discussion turned to the formation of a petition, to be sent to city hall about Mrs. Wary's property, Jonathan sprang into action. People chuckled when a stool was placed in front of the microphone, but they did not laugh for long.

In the loudest, most serious voice he could generate, Jonathan told everyone that Mrs. Wary was his friend and had lived in this neighbourhood longer than anyone else. That she was an important person, who had taught many in the community, as a former teacher. Her yard was a haven for birds and bees that pollinated every other garden for miles around the area. Her home was full of antiques and historic stories about their subdivision that would be lost without her. She helps many students demystify difficult school work, not just for himself, but another kid his age, named Billy. How he witnessed adults bullying Mrs. Wary by being unfriendly and spreading negative gossip behind her back. That these new urban plans would only pit people against one another and unjustly judge individuals. This neighbourhood renewal was just bullying in disguise.

Everyone went silent as a moment of discomfort settled over the room. Jonathan did not know what to think but was just glad he got that off his chest. His father quickly stepped behind him and patted him on the back as someone exclaimed *"out of the mouth of babes!"*. Then one lone person started to quietly clap and as more joined in, the applause grew louder at the same time others silently got up and left. A few came up to the microphone to agree with the young man who spoke. Later his father said that he and his mother had shared the same concerns for the neighbourhood and Mrs. Wary. They were just not sure how to approach it without taking sides, becoming involved and making enemies. Jonathan's very grown up words, spoken with the innocence of someone with no invested interest, other than doing what is right, was exactly what their community needed to hear.

News of what happened spread quickly. The urban planning fizzled out. People were too ashamed to pick on Mrs. Wary, or any of the other residents, anymore. "Live and Let Live" became a new motto for neighbours, now on their best behaviour, after being outed by Jonathan. Mrs. Wary thanked Jonathan and reminded him that despite the lies marching out front, the truth always quietly brings up the rear. She also told him how important it was to find the good in others, as per her family motto.

The storms Jonathan had feared in his personal and social life, for the past several months, had finally dissipated. He was starting a new school in the fall and had grown more confident in his ability to navigate climate crises of a personal nature. His father and mother were proud of him and started involving him in adult discussions. He was no longer just a kid in trouble with his mother. All would be well after all.

ABOUT THE AUTHOR

SG Williams is a wellness specialist, author and publisher who previously spent decades working in science, research, technology, traditional holistic healing and acupuncture. She believes in simplicity, authenticity, the need to find inner peace and keeping the wonder of life alive by paying attention to our surroundings. She sees every person as unique and specially created with something important to teach us. In her opinion it is imperative for everyone to have access to healthy communities, where people can be appreciated for who they are, free from injustice and discrimination.

www.ingramcontent.com/pod-product-compliance
Lightning Source LLC
Chambersburg PA
CBHW070606050426
42450CB00011B/3002